THE GALLEY
K·I·S·S·
COOKBOOK

By Corinne C. Kanter

 **Author of
CORINNE'S
CULINARY
CORNER**

Inquiries should be addressed to:
Corinne C. Kanter
SAILco Press,
P.O. Box 2099
Key Largo, FL 33037

Tel & Fax (305)743-0626
email: kisscook@sailcopress.com

visit our website at:
http://www.charternet.com/greatgear/greatbooks

First printing. . . June, 1987
Second Printing . . . November, 1990
Third Printing . . . June, 1992
Fourth Printing . . . October, 1993
Fifth Printing . . . July, 1995
REVISED Sixth Printing . . . June, 1998

Library of Congress Catalog Card Number: 87-90534
ISBN: 0-9618406-0-9

$13.95

Printed in the United States of America

DEDICATION

To Chuck — who encouraged me to go for it. Who patiently waited for me as I rowed back from boats in my dinghy with one more recipe to share with others.

ACKNOWLEDGEMENTS

This book has been three years in the making. Charles Chiodi, Tristan Jones, Whitey Schmidt, Jan Robinson and Henry Wagner all implored me to publish the book myself. They were my strength throughout the ordeal of learning how to do it. Without them and the myriad cruising friends, contributors, avid column readers and my family this book would not have been possible.

ODE TO THE DIETER

Cholesterol is poisonous. So never, never eat it.
Sugar, too, may murder you; there is no way to beat it.
And fatty food may do you in; be certain to avoid it.
Some food was rich in vitamins but processing destroyed it.
So let your life be ordered by each documented fact.
And die of malnutrition — but with arteries intact.

Author Unknown

AUTHOR'S NOTE

Dear reader, let me attribute my eleven years of successful publishing to you. Thank you for your feedback and thank you for your continued support. Sharing the **K.I.S.S.** principle with you is my joy. In this revised issue I have kept the recipes which now have truly stood the test of time and updated the Helpful Hints sections to incorporate those items you most fervently desired. Time, technology and new equipment, equal new ways to accomplish old truths.

Far from being a "chore", cooking and providing wholesome food for my family and friends is a very satisfying and rewarding life experience. Cooking is enjoyable in my home, out camping or on our boat. It was aboard *La Forza*, our 32ft. catamaran sailing yacht that I truly fine-tuned the art of preparing "Delicious, Nutritious Economical and Convenient" meals.

It is not necessary to alter your basic eating preferences nor become a human can opener to go cruising. The tips, hints and recipes in this book will show you why. Basic to all my recipes and techniques are readily obtainable ingredients found even in little shops or "Supermercado's" in exotic ports of call or our marvelous supermarkets and health food stores here in the U.S.A.

Many of the recipes in this book are kindly donated favorite recipes of cruising folks that I met along the Intra-coastal Waterway, through the Bahamas and the Caribbean. In return for their proven recipes I created a hand-made needlepoint bookmark of their boats' name. The balance of the recipes are my own favorites.

Whether you are cruising, camping, or a busy person on the go, sharing these recipes, helpful hints on food, long term cruising helpful hints, and hints about provisioning, stowage, galley gear and gadgets gives me much of the pleasure and satisfaction of putting this cookbook together.

CORINNE - INTREPID HEROINE
OUTRAGEOUS COOK

Corinne C. Kanter

ooo

TABLE OF CONTENTS

TERMS USED IN COOKERY

Au Gratin - Baked or grilled foods sprinkled with cheese, bread-crumbs and browned in the oven.

Baste - Moistening the surface of food to prevent drying and enhance flavor.

Beat - Make a mixture smooth by stirring, whipping motion with a spoon or electric mixer.

Blanche - Remove skin by pouring boiling water or steam over them to prepare fruits or vegetables for canning.

Bouquet Garni - A bunch of sweet herbs (3 springs of parsley 2 of thyme, 1 of marjoram and a bay leaf) tied together, used to flavor soups, stews, remove before serving.

Bouillon - A clear soup stronger than broth but not as strong as consomme.

Bread - Coat with bread crumbs before cooking.

Caramel - Browned sugar syrup.

Chop - Cut into pieces about the size of peas.

Clarify - Make liquids clear by filtering as stock or broth.

Coat - Evenly cover food with crumbs, flour or a batter.

Coddle - Cook food in water just below the boiling point.

Cool - Remove from heat, let stand until room temperature.

Cream - Beat a mixture with a spoon until it becomes soft and smooth. When applied to combining shortening and sugar, the mixture is beaten till light and fluffy.

Cube - Cut into pieces that are the same size on each side. Larger than ½ inch.

Cut In - Mix shortening with dry ingredients using a pastry blender or two knives.

Compote - Fruit cooked slowly in syrup.

Croutons - Small cubes of fried bread or toast about ½ inch square.

Dice - Cut food into small cubes of uniform size and shape. Smaller than ¼ inch.

Dollop - To add a small amount, such as a scoop or spoonful, of a semi-liquid food to garnish another food.

Dot - Distribute small bits of food over another food.

Dust - Sprinkle foods lightly with sugar, flour, etc.

Fillets - Cut of meat or pieces of fish with skin and bone removed.

Flake - Break food lightly into small pieces.

Fold - To add ingredients gently to a mixture, using a spatula.

Fry - Cook in hot oil. To pan fry, cook food in a small amount of oil. To deep-fat fry, cook the food immersed in a large amount of oil.

Garnish - To decorate often with a sprig of parsley.

Glaze - Brush pastry, biscuits, or buns with liquid such as a beaten egg, milk, or water and sugar to give a hard finish.

Julienne - Cut vegetables, fruits, or meats into match-like strips.

Knead - Compressing the ball of dough with the heel of your hand.

Marinade - Oil, vinegar and herbs poured over steak or fish before grilling, as a tenderizer.

Peel - Remove the skin from a fruit or vegetable.

Purée - Pulp of mashed vegetables, thick soup, meat or fish pounded in a mortar, or passed through a sieve.

Sauté - Toss over a low flame in a saucepan with butter, pepper and salt.

Shred - Rub food on a shredder to form long narrow pieces.

Sift - Put dry ingredients through a sieve or sifter.

Simmer - Cook food in liquid over low heat.

Steam - Cook food using a small amount of water.

Stew - Simmer food slowly in a small amount of liquid.

Stir - Mix ingredients with a spoon in a circular motion.

Stir-fry - Cook food quickly in a small amount of hot oil, stirring constantly.

Toss - Mix ingredients lightly by lifting and dropping them with a spoon, or a pair of chopsticks.

Whip - Beat food lightly and rapidly.

BASIC GROCERIES TO HAVE ON HAND

- baking powder, baking soda
- beans: canned and dried
- biscuit mix, (the mix contains yeast and baking soda, it will take the place of a large quantity of flour for baking)
- breads, biscuits, cookies
- butter
- canned beef, chicken, turkey, salmon, sardines, tuna, oysters, shrimp, ham, roast beef, corned beef, hash, clams
- crackers, assorted
- cheese: assorted, vacuum packed and some that need no refrigeration
- chocolate chips
- cinnamon
- coffee: instant, ground
- cocoa powder, baking chocolate
- dried onion flakes, parsley, bell pepper, mushroom
- eggs: fresh, powdered
- flour: all-purpose, whole wheat, bread
- fruit: (canned) small sizes crushed pineapple, pineapple chunks, applesauce, pears, peaches, apricots.
assortment of canned fruit pie filling
dried fruit: raisins, apricots, pineapple, currants, figs
fresh lemons
- garlic: fresh, dried and minced in oil
- grains: couscous, bulgur, instant grits, cornmeal
- instant pudding and dessert packs
- jams, preserves, honey
- juices, (see *Helpful Hints On Food*)
- ketchup, mayonnaise, mustard (dried and prepared)
- macaroni, spaghetti, noodles
- milk: evaporated, powdered, shelf-life
- mushrooms: canned and dried
- nuts: salted and unsalted

- onions: fresh
- peanut butter: crunchy, smooth
- pepper: ground, whole
- rice: instant, raw
- salt: sea, kosher
- small containers of: herbs, sauces, seasonings
- snacks: popcorn, pretzels, individual candy bars, trail mix, chips, hard candy, cookies, your favorite snacks (great for night watches or a special celebration)
- soups: canned, dried
- soy sauce
- sugar: brown, granulated, powdered
- tomatoes: fresh, paste, puree, stewed, sauces
- oils: extra virgin olive oil, peanut, canola oil
- tea: assortment
- vinegar: red wine, rice, balsamic, cider
- yeast: granular

ADDITIONAL GROCERIES

- anchovies, pimentos
- bacon: canned, dried, bits
- baking chocolate
- bean sprouts (canned)
- beverages: ginger ale, cola, alcoholic drinks, mixers
- cabbage
- cake, cookie and muffin mixes
- dry salami, pepperoni
- cornstarch
- flour, self rising flour
- fruits: fresh, canned, dried
- horseradish, pickles, olives, relishes, artichokes,
- potatoes: fresh, instant, yams
- salad dressings, chili, Worcestershire and hot sauce
- seeds for sprouting
- seeds: sunflower, pumpkin, pine nuts
- soups: condensed, instant, bouillon cubes, freeze dried
- syrup: maple, pancake)
- vegetables: fresh, dried, canned
- water chestnuts
- wheat germ

Here's my list of spices and seasonings:

All Spice	Cinnamon	Oregano
Basil	Cumin	Paprika
Bay Leaf	Curry	Parsley Flakes
Cardamon	Dill	Rosemary
Celery Salt	Dry Mustard	Saffron
Chili Powder	Ginger	Sesame Seeds
Cloves,ground	Lemon Pepper	Tarragon
Chives,dried	Onion Flakes	Thyme
Cilantro	Nutmeg	Vanilla

Provisioning For Long Term Cruising

*The following **FRESH** foods store well for long periods of time. Example: a month cruise for two adults, occasional guests, **without any reprovisioning.***

- 4 dozen eggs, for eating, baking, cooking
- 24 tomatoes, mixture of green to red
- 24 carrots
- 6 green peppers (wrap in wax pepper)
- 12 squashes, mix variety, potatoes, yams
- 24 bananas in various stages of green to ripe
- 5 plantains, select very bright green to dark
- 3 garlic heads
- 2 medium hard cabbage
- 6 pounds of yellow onions
- 2 large red onions
- 1 celery
- 12 fresh lemons
- 3 limes
- 1 Daikon radish

FRESH foods to be eaten first

- 2 large heads of lettuce
- 1 broccoli, cauliflower, (each)
- 2 eggplants
- 2 cucumbers or 6 pickling cukes
- 6 pears, apples
- 1 pineapple
- 6 kiwi fruits, select hard to one ripe
- 12 grapefruits
- 12 oranges

❍❍❍❍❍❍❍❍❍❍❍❍❍❍❍❍❍❍❍❍❍❍❍❍❍❍❍❍❍❍❍❍❍❍❍❍❍❍

For a cruise of at least one month the quantities of BASIC items that I purchase are listed below. These quantities are figured for two adults, occasional guests. For those with special diets, substitute accordingly.

Note: If you are going to the Bahamas some items are actually less expensive than in the U.S. Some of theses are: Canadian flour, bulk cheese, whipping cream in a can, canned non-refrigerated butter, English tea.

Some items like paper goods, U.S. produced foodstuffs and coffee are dramatically higher in price. You will be able to purchase some local tomatoes, cabbage, green peppers, limes. The Dominican Republic has a profusion of vegetables at low prices. Puerto Rico has plenty of supermarkets at prices about like the U.S.

- 2 pounds regular coffee
- 1 jar instant coffee
- 48 tea bags
- 2 (1 lb.) canned ham
- 2 packages of sprouting beans
- 24 cans of assorted cooked canned beans, red kidney, black, garbanzo, lima beans. These can be used as a side dish, or tossed together for a bean salad.
- 6 cans each of kernel corn, beets, stewed tomatoes, asparagus
- 6 small cans sauerkraut
- 6 packages dried lentils and green-pea
- 12 cans assorted: fish, chicken or turkey, beef, shrimp, clams, corned beef
- 10 packages of assorted cheese vacuum-packed, non-refrigerated, waxed
- 1 gallon cooking oil
- 1 large bottle of extra virgin olive oil
- 2 bottles of vinegar: red wine, balsamic
- 2 jars of peanut butter
- 2 jars of jelly or jam
- 4 (6 oz.) packages of freeze-dried egg yolks (see helpful hints)
- 2 cans of Brown bread
- 1 large box oatmeal

- Butter, four pounds
- Condiments, mayonnaise, mustard, relish, pickles
- 24 single serving cans or bottles: soda, juices, V-8, grapefruit, orange, prune
- 6 containers of juice concentrate
- 3 containers of instant powder fruit juice
- 12 assorted packages of flavored rice
- 4 pounds of variety rice: Basmati, Jasmine, long grain, precooked
- 2 pounds each: couscous, bulgur, kasha
- 4 pounds assorted pastas
- 6 cans of tomato paste
- 6 jars of spaghetti sauce
- 4 cans of whole tomatoes
- 1 large package of tortillas
- 24 cans of assorted fruits
- 3 pounds assorted dried fruit
- 12 ready to eat pudding or dessert packs

BASIC SUPPLIES

- aluminum foil, plastic wrap, wax paper
- bleach, scouring powder
- cheesecloth, coffee filters
- funnel for stove and lamp fuels
- sturdy garbage bags, various sizes
- matches, long nose butane lighter
- paper products: towels, tissue, toilet, plates, hot and cold cups
- steel wool pads and soap pads
- toothpicks, candles
- dustpan with brush, mop, clothespins
- soap (Joy detergent works in sea water)

○○○○○○○○○○○○○○○○○○○○○○○○○○○○○○○○○○○○○○

GALLEY GEAR AND GADGETS

When I hear the Captain grumble, "look at the water-line of this boat", I tell him to either raise the water-line or eat fast and drink the beer. Then watch it eventually return to normal. However, to be a little more practical I have concluded that whatever is brought on board, galley gear and gadgets included, must have more than one use.

LIST OF POTS, PANS, GADGETS

My set of pots are super high-tech, being truly "stickless", therefore, using precious little water for cleaning. The lids have a small vent in them to relieve pressure without opening the lid. This makes for less steam in the galley and for not worrying about a partially opened lid sliding off when a wake goes by. My set consists of a large skillet, Dutch oven, one medium and one small saucepan. When purchasing your set, It's important to lift the pots in your hands to see if you feel comfortable with them.

In addition to the above list, here is my total utensil list:

- can opener
- cheese slicer
- chopsticks: 6 pair
- cookie sheets, (2) with sides
- containers: assorted sizes
- combination cork screw-/bottle opener
- cutting boards: 1 large, one small (see Helpful Hints)
- dinnerware: my service for 6 is Corelle, lightweight, easy to clean, stacks very well, chip resistant, comes in a variety of patterns. (see Helpful Hints, plastic containers)
- stainless-steel flatware: a complete service for 6
- large mugs (4), 6 wine glasses

- 2 large insulated mugs with sealable tops
- funnel for potable liquids
- garlic press
- grater (four sided)
- ice pick
- knives: chef's, filet, paring, boning, bread, serrated slicer
- loaf baking pans (2)
- measuring cups and spoons
- meat thermometer
- mixing bowls: set of 3 nesting in one another, (double as serving bowls)
- muffin tin (1)
- paint brushes (used as a pastry brush)
- pie tin
- pot holders: 1 mitt, 2 squares
- poultry shears
- pressure cooker (see Helpful Hints)
- roasting pan
- tea kettle (see Helpful Hints)
- tenderizer hammer (wood)
- timer
- trays, variety of shapes and sizes
- utensils: soup ladle, slotted spoon, large fork, spatula
- vacuum bottles: 2 (see Helpful Hints)
- vegetable brush, peeler and steamer
- whisk
- wire rack, for cooling cakes, breads and cookies

HELPFUL HINTS ON FOOD

APPLES: Wash before storing to get rid of any potential pests and insecticides. Dry well and wrap in tissue paper. Place in open crate and store in a cool dark area. Great for pies, salads, and just a quick pick-up munch.

AVOCADOS: Avocados can be bought in many stages of firmness so they ripen at different periods of time.

BAY LEAVES: Discourages weevils, "the pets from H--l," Store flour, rice, grains, pastas, beans in air-tight containers, place a couple of bay leaves inside. The bay leaves keep those critters away.

BEANS: Canned: green, lima, garbanzo, pinto, black and red kidney beans. Not only do you have the makings of a bean salad, but you have vegetables that can be added to cooked stew, or clear broth soup.
Dried: lentils, split pea, lima bean, northern bean, pigeon peas. Make your own mixture of dried beans for a great bean soup. Store them in an air-tight container.

BEVERAGES: Your choice for alcoholic and non-alcoholic drinks. In foreign countries soda pop is quite expensive. If your into gin and tonic, stock up on the tonic water. Liquors can be inexpensive depending on the brand. Take along your favorite wines. In general you will be able to enjoy local beer, rum and wine.

BREAD: Preserve a fresh supply of bread. Buy loaves unsliced, lightly wipe them down with white vinegar, wrap in plastic wrap, and place in resealable bag. Stays nice and fresh for a long period of time. Save stale bread, use it for croutons, French toast and stuffing or to feed the friendly local ducks. Canned date-nut bread needs no refrigeration. Serve at that special meal, or along with a hearty breakfast. It comes in handy when your fresh bread is gone.

BONES: Don't discard that baked ham bone, roasted turkey breast. They make a great base for your homemade soup.

BUTTER: Canned butter from New Zealand generally can be found in the island stores as well as health-food stores in the USA.
•If you would like to store fresh butter before shoving off, do the following: Boil water and add 1 tablespoon salt to each quart of boiled water, let cool down. Clean and sterilize glass jars and fill about ¾ full with sticks of butter, add boiled water and salt mixture on top. Close tightly and store in a cool place, the butter will last a long time.

CABBAGE: Stores well without refrigeration in a netted bag. Red or green, use alone or as a combination, in coleslaw, soups, stir-fry and stuffed cabbage. Use it instead of lettuce.

CHEESE: Select an assortment of cheeses, vacuum packed, wax coated which require no refrigeration. When your cheese becomes dried and hard, don't discard it. Grate and store in an airtight container. Use it for salads, soups, vegetable toppings or in casserole dishes. Wrap a piece of cheesecloth moistened with vinegar around the hard cheese to keep it fresh.

CINNAMON SUGAR: Use a small container for 1 cup white sugar, 1 tablespoon ground cinnamon. Stir thoroughly and you will have cinnamon sugar ready on hand to use on pancakes, French toast, waffles, etc. instead of syrup.

CLAMS: Clams in cans come minced or chopped and used for a variety of dishes such as soups, cracker or vegetable spreads, or in a sauce with pasta. Clams can be substituted for conch. Chewy is chewy, don't tell them.

CONDENSED SOUPS: Use for bisques, broths, and casseroles. Choose celery, mushroom, clear broth, asparagus and tomato.
●To make a quick chicken egg drop soup do the following. Take one egg per four cups of soup and beat well. Pour the beaten egg slowly, a teaspoon full at a time, into a pot of boiling chicken noodle soup or clear chicken broth, cook until egg sets, then serve. If you want the soup a little thick, make a smooth paste of cornstarch and water, slowly add this to the boiling soup, stirring until the soup reaches the desired thickness.

DEHYDRATED and FREEZE DRIED FOODS: These foods are lightweight, packed in waterproof packs. Select a variety of foods for breakfast, dinner, desserts, soups, sauces, bread and pancake mixes. Purchase dried tomatoes, bell pepper, garlic chips. Select a variety of dried fruits. Available in supermarkets and health food stores.

∘⊂∘

EGGS: Fresh eggs will keep without refrigeration about three weeks with just normal care. If you grease eggs with vegetable shortening and place right back in their cartons and store in a cool place you can extend their shelf life another three weeks. Some people use petroleum jelly to coat eggs. I like shortening myself, it's easier to apply. Turn eggs upside down in their containers every 2 or 3 days to keep the yolks suspended, especially in the tropics. Keep 2 or 3 hard cooked eggs on hand to add to tuna, chicken, salmon, or ham salad spreads. Cut a hard boiled egg up into a fresh vegetable salad.

FLOUR: *All-purpose flour* is a mixture of hard-wheat and soft-wheat and comes bleached and unbleached.
Unbleached is a flour that has not been bleached or had maturing agents added.
Other types of flour are pastry, semolina, gluten, graham and cake. Read the specific instructions and uses for each on the package labels.
Self-rising flour is just all-purpose flour with baking powder and salt added to it. It is used primarily for biscuits, muffins, and other quick breads. To make self-rising flour, add ½ teaspoon salt and 1½ teaspoons baking powder to 1 cup of all-purpose flour.
Bread flour is made of the hardest wheat flours, which are generally considered most suitable for bread baking and pasta making.
Whole wheat flour makes a bread easily sliced for sandwiches or toast.

FRUITS: DRIED, CANNED: Dried: Carry a variety of figs, dates, raisins, apples and tropical fruit.
Canned: becomes a dessert, a starter for breakfast or just a quick snack. Quick dessert add your favorite brandy or rum topped with whipping cream.

GINGER: Spicy and hot in taste. Look for plump but firm pieces of Ginger root, light tan in color, with a tight skin. You can store peeled ginger in a glass jar of sherry or vodka for several months. Candied ginger is said to be great for seasickness as are ginger snap cookies.

INSTANT POWDER DRINKS, CONCENTRATE: Take along a good variety of powdered fruit drink mixes and small juice concentrate packs such as apple, cranberry, etc. There's less weight on board, easy to use and come in small plastic containers which are easy to store.

INSTANT CUP OF SOUP, INSTANT DESSERT: These come in handy when heavy weather hits or just for a quick picker upper snack. They can be bought in case lots. Select instant pudding, dessert six packs.

LEMONS: For maximum storage time, wrap individually in aluminum foil and store in cool dark ventilated area.

MILK: I use a great powdered whole milk: *Nestlé "NIDO"*. Powdered milk is used not only for a beverage, but in everyday cooking or for instant puddings. Once the tin is opened use as needed, requires no refrigeration. *Nestlé* also makes non-refrigerated whipping cream which is great for the Fettuccine recipes. Shelf life milk, once opened requires refrigeration. *Saco* cultured buttermilk blend in powder concentrate, is good for cooking and baking. It comes in a 12 oz. container. Use it for making your scratch pancakes, biscuits, bread recipes and buttermilk dressings.

ooo

ONIONS: Store in a cool dark well ventilated area away from contact with other fruits or vegetables. Vidalia onions must be kept cool, dry and separate. Use the legs of old, clean sheer pantyhose. Tie a knot between each onion, cut above the knot when you want an onion.

PLANTAIN: Purchased very hard and bright green in color. When fully ripened (black skin) slice thin and sauté in butter, drizzle honey on top and serve.

SAUERKRAUT: Purchase small cans of sauerkraut to top off your hot dogs or use in a Reuben sandwiches.

SAUSAGE: There are several brands of smoked sausage that need no refrigeration. They come packaged in vacuum sealed wrappings. Use in casserole dishes, toppings on pizza, or as a appetizers with cheese slices.

SQUASH: Acorn, Banana, Bohemian, Buttercup, Butternut, Hubbards, Kabocha, Pumpkin, Spaghetti and Turban, store in a cool dark area, they keep up to six months. Thin skinned squash should be wrapped in tissue paper. All are stored in a netted hammock or open crate.

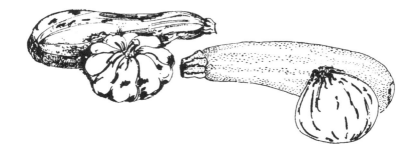

SPROUTERS & SPROUTS: I don't need to describe how nice it is to have fresh veggies every day. The next best thing is to get you to grow sprouts.

• If you don't have a three tier sprouter a paper plate will do. Place beans for sprouting on the paper plate. Cover with a paper towel soaked in water but not dripping, sprinkle water on the towel twice a day for three days and your beans will sprout well. Instead of a paper plate you can use a empty mayonnaise jar with cheesecloth top to drain the excess water out. Lay it on its side when using. Various beans and seeds for easy sprouting: alfalfa, wheat, lentils, radish take 2-3 days to sprout. Mung sprouts in 3-4 days.

Paper plate

Mayonnaise jar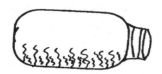

Three-tier sprouter

TOMATOES: Purchase tomatoes in various stages of ripe to almost ripe. Store the green ones in a brown paper bag, they will slowly turn red. Eat the red ones as they ripen.

VEGETABLES, Canned: Stewed tomatoes, zucchini, spinach, squash, black beans, kernel corn, asparagus, garbanzo, beets, and lima beans are just a few of the vegetables that have a great taste coming out of a can. Select small size cans.

VEGETABLES, Fresh: Some fresh vegetables that keep for long periods of time in a dark, cool area are butternut, acorn and spaghetti squash, yams, and Irish potatoes.

WHEAT GERM: Wheat Germ: comes flaked, coarse-ground, raw or toasted. Use it when making homemade granola, crunch in a bread recipe, or to coat fresh fish, chicken or chops.

○◇○◇○◇○◇○◇○◇○◇○◇○◇○◇○◇○◇○◇○◇○◇○◇○◇○◇○

Long Term Cruising???

HELPFUL HINTS

This section is for you intrepid cruisers who would like to share some of my experiences, trials and tribulations that I have boiled down into a series of what I call "helpful hints". These hints are randomly listed by topic and cover the broad range of skills needed for tranquil cruising.

GUESTBOOK: I have one guest book on board for visitors to sign in. You may want to have a large index file for your permanent records or put it in the computer. I usual cross reference my files by using the boat's name (with vital information) as well as the persons name. OR you may want to keep a large scrapbook, take a instant Polaroid picture, paste the instant photo on a page. Then your guest signs in under their picture instantly, creating a permanent memory for you.

ONE-BURNER STOVE TOP: Try the *Kenyon* **KISS** stove, check their website **http://www.kenyonmarine.com**

LAUNDRY BAGS: Use sturdy canvas laundry bags. Two large bags, one for bath towels and linen, the other for clothing. One small bag for galley towels, so when it's time to do the laundry, it's already sorted. Make sure you keep a good supply of quarters, dimes and nickels for the washers and dryers.

PAINT BRUSHES: Purchase the assorted sizes package of paint brushes and turn them into your pastry and BBQ brushes. They clean much easier in soap and water and cost less.

∞∞∞∞∞∞∞∞∞∞∞∞∞∞∞∞∞∞∞∞∞∞∞∞∞∞∞∞∞∞∞∞∞

LINENS: I carry three complete set of sheets, and a few extra pillow cases on board. I also carry light-weight terry bath towels, which are much easier to wring out by hand when washing machines aren't available. We use small hand terry towels (12) for our daily napkins and keep them tucked into their own napkin holder.

PLASTIC BAGS: I use resealable bags in small, medium and large sizes. In the small ones, I store the quick treats needed when alone on those long dark watches. I place a full meal in a large bag for those quick grab, heat and eat meals. To save bags, I first repack all of the food that comes in cardboard packaging into the inexpensive plastic bags you find in the vegetable department section of the supermarket. This saves getting the resealable bags dirty. Place the label of contents of the food and the cooking instructions inside between the two bags.

TRASH: The disposal dilemma: I'm quoting a dear friend, cruiser *Liza Copeland*. "When provisioning for a cruise, the amount of trash that will accrue can be greatly reduced by removing unnecessary packaging prior to departure." Items such as flour, rice, cake mixes, breakfast cereals, herbs, and cookies can be stowed in robust air-tight and reusable containers. Follow U.S. and international pollution guidelines.

ALOE PLANT: This plant grows very easily in a small pot with limited sunlight. Besides its beauty it helps heal cuts, burns, bruises. It is world renowned for anything to do with the skin. Take one along and as it multiplies give a sprout to a friend.

‐‐‐‐‐‐‐‐‐‐‐‐‐‐‐‐‐‐‐‐‐‐‐‐‐‐‐‐‐‐‐‐‐‐‐‐

TENDERIZER: Many people use Papaya extract meat tenderizer on sea nettle stings and insect bites. Sprinkle on and away goes that itch and sting.

ICE CUBES: Plastic ice cube bags are simple to use and simple to store in the freezer. There are 10 disposable plastic bags inside one package, that's 180 ice cubes. Each bag makes 18 cubes. Fill through built-in funnel, double tie and freeze. *Scubs Consumer Products Inc.*, Grand Island, NY 14072 or a chandlery. Fill with not only water but fruit juice or ice tea. Store your home-made clear cooled soup stock, pop out a cube of stock at a time.

INSULATED SOFT COOLERS: These come in a variety of sizes. I use the small size for all important ship papers, etc. kept at the companionway on our overnight crossings (they float). The medium size as an emergency food pack. Once you arrive at your destination this insulated bag can keep things cold while shopping until you return to the boat. The large bag holds a block of ice for 3-4 days. This will keep lots of cold drinks cold without going into the main refrigerator. When drinks are gone this soft-pack bag can stow away easily unlike bulky hard large size coolers.

STORAGE HINT: Make a diagram of your storage spaces. I have two spaces on *La Forza*. One is my heavy supply and the other my every-day condiments and light fares. I keep an inventory sheet marked off in columns as to the quantity I start with, location of item and a column as I remove an item. When I reprovision, I have an accurate count of my stores on board. It's frustrating trying to remember where that particular item is, when you start or are in the middle of making a dish. Stock up on staples and favorites. Part of the adventure of cruising is sampling/shopping the cuisines of new and different cultures.

PLASTIC CONTAINERS: Go to your local restaurants and get friendly with the Chef. Ask for the large plastic containers with lids (they get mayonnaise, salad dressings, relishes in them) use these for storing flour, rice, oatmeal, pastas, biscuit mix, noodles, etc. They also have larger 12 quart hard containers with lids which can be used for substitute buckets. Set aside two for wash days when a laundromat isn't available. These large buckets are great for scooping up water from cisterns. Turn a Tupperware cake holder upside down and it will store a complete service for 4 of Corelle dishes safely.

ICE STRETCHER: Two nights before going away for the weekend, place your favorite fruit drink or drinking water in plastic re-useable clean milk containers and freeze. Pack instead of ice in your softpack insulated bag, chest or refrigerator. Your frozen drink will keep other items cold, as it defrosts and you get truly cold drinks as a bonus, instead of dealing with that wasted melted ice.

HAMPERS: We use small plastic hampers 18" X 24", they have a hinged lid and ventilated holes on one side. They hold our linen and towel supply and also double as an extra seat or coffee table and foot stool.

VACUUM BOTTLES: Carry two vacuum bottles. Each morning I brew my coffee directly into one bottle, the second bottle holds the remaining hot water to be used later on in the day. Saves cooking fuel, water, time.

CUTTING BOARDS: Use one side of a large wood cutting board for fresh vegetables, the other side for slicing cooked foods. One small cutting board for ONLY raw foods. Wash each board often with a solution of bleach and water.

PRESSURE COOKER: Out of the past and into the future with the versatility of the pressure cooker. Today's busy, nutrition-conscious cooks find the pressure cooker convenient, economical (they save water, fuel and time, keeps heat out of the cabin, has a large safety margin since they have locking tops); and they make wholesome dishes. I am presently using a 6-quart stainless steel *FAGOR* Pressure Cooker. The important features on this cooker are: Two short handles to lift pot, being able to release pressure without waiting for it to come down of its own accord or using cold water to bring pressure down. You can even deep fry under pressure with this cooker. This cooker can be purchased at major boat shows or send for information to *Show-Me Products*, 1125 32nd. St. N., Texas City, TX 77590, 409-948-4457.

ROLYKIT OR TACKLE BOX: The rolykit compact box unrolls to 6 feet long and has many adjustable compartments for storage of small items.
Tackle boxes come in many sizes and stages of waterproof. Turn one into your own first aid kit. Use one for radio and electronic parts, nuts, bolts, sewing supplies or any other small hard to find or store items.

PAPER: Paper products in the USA are very inexpensive, so before you sail away from it all, stock up on toilet paper, paper towels and tissues. Practice being as conservative as possible with them, because in the foreign countries they cost about three times what they do here.

● To make ordinary paper towels last twice as long, I cut them in half before putting them on the paper towel holder. Be sure the factory edges face one another. There are so many times when half a sheet will do.

FRESH WATER SPRAY: To help conserve your fresh water supply, wash dishes in salt water whenever it's clean enough and rinse with fresh. Use a plastic bottle with a hand pump spray head, filled with fresh water, spray rinse dishes or whatever needs it. Please follow U.S. and international pollution guidelines. For those of you who will be carrying additional containers of fresh water, don't get too large a size. They will be easier to handle, especially when full and lifting from dinghy to the boat topsides.

TOTE IT: Fanny packs leave your hands free and they stay safely attached to you. The modern lightweight back pack is a boon to shoppers as well as travelers. Take them with you to the stores they greatly simplify toting home the grub.

TEA KETTLE: The tea kettle is a very important piece of equipment used daily. I am mentioning the brand name, because of its durability, good handle, spout and **SAFETY** design. You fill the kettle and pour the hot boiling water out of the same spout. Some tea kettles are cute looking, but often dangerous. Accidents happen from the handle pivoting or the top falling off. I have the larger *Revere Ware* teakettle, its single-opening trigger operated spout and fixed handle is a basic design that hasn't changed in years. I'm glad, because it is functional and SAFE!

CANNED FOODS: There are lots of quality along with variety of good canned foods. If some are new to you, try a small size first before stocking up on it. In addition try purchasing a variety of sizes. There will be times when a small size can will do.

FOLDING BIKES: A pair of 20" folding bikes are our main means of shoreside transportation and we wouldn't be without them. Installed on both sides of the rear tire are saddle bags made out of Textilene material (water runs through easily if it rains). On a carrier over the rear fender one can clip on an open plastic milk carton to carry additional supplies. The bikes have a light generated by pedal power and a bell attached to the handlebars. Reflectors on the pedals and rear fender. It's a great way to go around in town, do your shopping, explore new areas.

CLAY FLOWER POT HEATER: For those cold evenings on board if you do not have heater or other type of warming device, take along a clean clay flower pot. Turn the pot upside down, set on the top burner of your stove. Heat red hot. Turn burner to low, allowing the heat escape into the cabin directly from the **HOT** clay pot. The pot actually becomes a clay refractory. Make sure you have good ventilation when doing this. **DO NOT** go to bed with the burner on.

PILLOWS, BLANKETS: Carry two extra pillows aside from sleeping, they become good backrests. Place them in some pretty pillowcases and leave them out for show. When traveling in cold climates, get two sleeping bags that can be zipped together, creating a large double size bag. Then sew two flat sheets on three sides tuck into zipped sleeping bag. This way when washing day comes, pull out soiled sheet for washing, which enables you to cut down on washing the bulky sleeping bags. In warm climates I like to use the open weave cotton blanket, they are lightweight, easy to launder.

Appetizers

∞∞∞∞∞∞∞∞∞∞∞∞∞∞∞∞∞∞∞∞∞∞∞∞∞∞∞∞∞∞∞

SWISS SPINACH QUICHE

1 can buttermilk biscuit (or your favorite unbaked pie crust)
8 ounces Swiss cheese, cut into strips
2 tablespoons flour
1 cup milk
3 eggs, beaten
½ teaspoon salt
¼ teaspoon nutmeg
10 ounces chopped spinach, drained
dash pepper

Toss Swiss cheese and flour and put into unbaked pie shell. If you are using buttermilk biscuits, place biscuits down in ungreased pie pan and press together forming a pie shell. In small bowl, mix milk, eggs, seasonings, then add spinach, pour over cheese and bake 350° 40-50 minutes. Serve warm.

CHEESE STRAWS
from Jonni DeWeerdt aboard "Seeker"

4 ounces (½ cup) grated Cheddar cheese
2 tablespoons soft butter
½ cup flour
½ teaspoon Worcestershire sauce
¼ teaspoon salt
2 drops hot pepper sauce

Blend all the above ingredients well. Roll dough to ¼" thickness. Cut 3" x ½" straws. Place on ungreased cookie sheet. Bake in hot oven 425°, approximately 11 minutes. Makes 2 dozen.

○○○○○○○○○○○○○○○○○○○○○○○○○○○○○○○○○○○○

MUSHROOM-BLUE CHEESE QUICHE
from Norma Henderson aboard "Cera"

1 shortcrust 9″ pastry shell, uncooked
½ pound mushrooms
1 tablespoon lemon juice
¼ cup blue cheese, crumbled
4 scallions, chopped
3 strips bacon, crumbled
3 eggs
½ cup milk
¼ cup half and half
dash pepper and salt

Make a shortcrust pastry and line a 9″ pie tin. Cook mushrooms and lemon juice until dryish. Pour this mixture into pie shell along with blue cheese, scallions, and bacon. In a separate bowl lightly beat the remaining ingredients and add to pie shell. Cook in hot oven for 45 minutes or until brown and puffy.

CHEDDAR CHEESE CRISPS

1 cup all purpose flour
½ cup butter
½ cup Cheddar cheese, grated
½ teaspoon salt

In medium bowl work butter, cheese, flour and salt with your hands, until a soft dough. Roll on floured surface and make long strips. Cut into 1½′ strips and place on lightly greased cookie sheet. Bake 400° 7-10 minutes or golden brown. Serve.

STUFFED CLAMS ALA MARIAH
from Terry Gott aboard "Mariah"

2 cups chopped clams and juice
salt and pepper to taste
2 tablespoons oil
2 tablespoons thyme
2 tablespoons oregano
2 tablespoons grated Parmesan cheese
Italian flavor bread crumbs
2 strips bacon cut into 1" pieces, uncooked
paprika for topping

Either purchase empty shells in variety store, or get some from your local seafood restaurant. Combine all ingredients except bacon and paprika. Stuff clam shells, sprinkle top with paprika and place a small piece of bacon on top. Place filled shells on cookie sheet in oven and bake at 350° until bacon is cooked. Serve with wedges of lemon.

CRISPY CONCH STRIPS
from Angela Wellman aboard "Suffolk Punch"

2-3 cleaned conch
3 tablespoons Reallime or fresh lime juice
½ cup flour
½ teaspoon salt
½ teaspoon pepper
½ teaspoon paprika

Slice and pound conch, then cut into long strips and place in a small bowl. Marinate with lime juice for at least 1 hour, then drain. Shake strips in a bag containing the seasoned flour until well coated. Place individual strips in hot oil and fry until crispy golden on one side, turn over till brown all over, drain and serve immediately. Good with red pepper sauce or cocktail sauce.

LA FORZA CONCH FRITTERS

4-5 medium conch
2 large onions, grated
½ green pepper, diced
1 cup flour
½ tablespoon baking powder
½ cup evaporated milk
salt, pepper, thyme

Clean conch, grind or chop in fine pieces. Add all remaining ingredients. This mixture should be slightly thick but drops off of spoon easily. Drop by teaspoon into hot oil 2″ deep in small frying pan. Turn fritter over after first side has fried to a golden brown and do the same for the other side. Serve with your favorite hot or cocktail sauce.

HOT CRAB YOGURT APPETIZER

1 (3 ounce) package cream cheese
1 small can crabmeat
½ cup blue cheese
1 egg, beaten
½ cup white wine
½ cup mayonnaise
½ cup yogurt

Blend wine, cream and blue cheese in bowl. Add remaining ingredients, mix lightly and pour into medium size greased casserole. Bake 375° for 25 minutes. Serve with your favorite crackers.

BAKED CLAMS ALA CATHERINE

from Jonnie DeWeerdt aboard "Seeker"

1 stick melted butter or margarine
1½ cups seasoned bread crumbs
2 teaspoons parsley
2 tablespoons Parmesan cheese
4 teaspoons lemon juice
1½ teaspoons oregano
1½ teaspoons garlic powder
2 teaspoons sherry wine
dash pepper
3 (8 ounce) cans minced clams, drained, reserve juice
1 can baby clams

Combine all above ingredients, mix thoroughly. Add enough juice to moisten. Stuff shells. When ready to serve sprinkle with olive oil and paprika, heat at 350° 20 minutes. Makes 50. Fresh clams are of course as good or better than the canned variety if you're around to get some. What a treat.

HOT CRABMEAT APPETIZER

from Joan Russell aboard "Maerdym"

1 (8 ounce) package cream cheese
1½ cups flaked drained crabmeat (7½ ounce can)
2 tablespoons finely chopped onion
2 tablespoons milk
½ teaspoon cream style horseradish
¼ teaspoon salt
dash pepper
⅓ cup sliced almonds, toasted

Combine all ingredients except nuts, mixing until well blended. Spoon into 9″ pie plate. Sprinkle with nuts. Bake 375° 15 minutes. This dip can be prepared in advance and baked just before serving. Delicious.

ooo

BARBECUE SAUSAGE BALLS
from Karen Anderson aboard "Harmony"

1 pound bulk pork sausage
1 egg
⅓ cup fine bread crumbs

Combine together and shape into 1″ balls. In skillet, brown on all sides, drain off grease. Set aside.

Sauce:
½ teaspoon sage
½ cup ketchup
1 tablespoon vinegar
1 tablespoon soy sauce
2 tablespoons brown sugar
1 teaspoon Tabasco sauce (or other hot sauce)

Mix sauce ingredients together in saucepan, heat. Pour over meat balls in skillet. Simmer for 30 minutes before serving.

BEER HOT DOGS
from Lois Walsh aboard "Pamlico Prowler"

1 pound package hot dogs, cut in bite size pieces
½ cup BBQ sauce
½ cup brown sugar
½ cup beer

Bring to boil all ingredients, then simmer for 3 minutes. Put in bowl and serve.

● ●

SUSHI ALA CHUCK

from Charles E. Kanter aboard "La Forza"

Filet your fresh catch of the day
1 package dry seaweed (purchase in health food store)
1 small amount of Japanese horseradish paste, set aside
1 cup cooked rice

Place seaweed on flat bamboo roll (or piece of plastic wrap). Top with cooked rice, a small amount of horseradish and fish, roll tightly and slice into bite size pieces. Place on platter, along with dish of soy sauce to dip sushi in.

CHUCK'S SASHIMI

from Charles E. Kanter aboard "La Forza"

Tuna is our favorite, but any fresh fish will do.
Slice filets into bite size pieces, slicing with the grain.
½ cup soy sauce
2 tablespoons water
3 tablespoons wasabi powder horseradish (Japanese horseradish), mix with a little bit of water to form a smooth paste
1 cup thinly sliced onions

On a large platter place the filet pieces of fish in center, in each small bowl place soy sauce mixture, horseradish mixture and sliced onions. To eat dip fish in soy sauce then paste, and pick up some onions. Use your chopsticks to eat with.

●●●

MUSHROOMS MARINADE

1 pound fresh mushrooms, washed and steamed until
   tender
2 tablespoons oregano
1 tablespoon basil
1 tablespoon Italian seasoning
2-3 cloves garlic, minced
½ cup tarragon vinegar
¾ cup olive oil

In mixing bowl add all ingredients, when mushrooms have
cooled down put into liquids and let marinate for 1-2 hours
before serving.

PICKLED EGGS

1 dozen eggs
1 cup vinegar
¼ cup water
¼ cup sugar
1 tablespoon dry mustard
1 teaspoon salt
1½ teaspoons celery seed
1 large onion, sliced
1 teaspoon mustard seed

Hard boil eggs and peel. Mix all ingredients except eggs,
onions, and place liquid mixture into a quart glass jar. Next
alternate eggs and onion slices. Cover tightly and place jar in
cool dark area for 2-3 days before eating. Enjoy.

ooo

DEVILED EGGS

6 hard cooked eggs
2 tablespoons mayonnaise
1 teaspoon regular mustard
dash salt, pepper, garlic powder
1 tablespoon pickle relish
dash hot sauce
dash Worcestershire sauce
paprika

Slice eggs in half. In medium size bowl scoop out egg yolks and mash. Add all remaining ingredients except paprika and stuff this mixture back into egg whites. Sprinkle with paprika. Chill and serve.

RED PEPPER MARINATE
from Bev Schu aboard "Admiral Tozzie"

6 red peppers
olive oil
crushed garlic
sweet basil

Broil peppers until charred on all sides. Remove from broiler and place in paper bag. Place in sink as bag will become damp. Close bag and let set 30 minutes. Then remove skin (peels right off) and seeds. Cut into strips and place 1 layer at a time in flat Tupperware container. Between each layer sprinkle with chopped garlic, sweet basil, lots of salt. When finished sprinkle top with small amount of olive oil. Longer it sets better it is.

CREAM CHEESE ROLL-UPS
from Betty Brock aboard "BJ III"

½ pound boiled ham
½ pound cream cheese
1 bunch scallions

Take a slice of boiled ham, spread with softened cream cheese and roll around a green onion top and all. Chill, slice not more than ½" wide. Serve.

FISH SALAD SPREAD
from Bev Schu aboard "Admiral Tozzie"

1 cup chopped cooked fish flakes
1 cup crisp cabbage, shredded
½ cup chopped celery
2 tablespoons chopped sweet pickles
½ teaspoon salt
⅛ teaspoon pepper
2 hard cooked eggs, chopped
2 tablespoons chopped onion
3-4 olives, chopped
½ green pepper, chopped
mayonnaise

Mix all ingredients except mayonnaise. Toss with mayonnaise to make spread. Can be served in bed of lettuce with crackers.

VELVEETA CHEESE SPREAD

from Mary Thomson aboard "Ringer's Rival II"

2 pounds Velveeta
8 ounces horseradish, do not drain
1 cup mayonnaise
½ jar Bacos

Melt cheese in double boiler, add mayonnaise and blend. Add horseradish blend some more. Add bacos, stir, put in jars. Will keep 3 weeks in refrigerator.

CURRIED TUNA SPREAD

from Sarah Tompson aboard "Sarasan"

1 can tuna
½ cup mayonnaise
1 can water chestnuts, chopped
1 cup celery, chopped
½ cup sharp Cheddar cheese, diced
1 small onion, chopped
1 tablespoon pickle relish
1 teaspoon prepared mustard
1-2 tablespoons curry powder (or more!)

Mix all above ingredients, serve on crackers or party rye. Best made a day ahead.

●◎●

JAMAICA PICKAPEPPA CONCH

from Anita Pyle aboard "Conch Quest"

1 large conch, cleaned
small dashes of lime juice, Pickapeppa sauce, salt
** and pepper to taste**

Slice a raw conch in thin slices (bite size). Combine lime juice, Jamaican Pickapeppa sauce, salt and pepper. Place conch in flat dish and pour mixture over adding thinly sliced onions. Marinate 2-3 hours and serve.

GUACAMOLE

3-4 ripe avocados
1 medium onion, chopped
1 tablespoon salt
1 teaspoon garlic powder
2 medium tomatoes, chopped
½ teaspoon hot sauce
3 tablespoons lemon juice

In mixing bowl, mash the avocados. Mix in onion, seasonings, tomato and lemon juice. Chill and serve with your favorite crackers or taco chips.

CLAM SPREAD

1 package cream cheese
2 small can clams, minced
1 small onion, grated
dash salt and pepper
dash hot sauce

Drain the clams. Mash the cheese and use some clam liquid to soften. Add remaining ingredients and blend well. Serve with crackers.

SHRIMP SPREAD

1 small can shrimp, cut in bite size pieces
1 hard cooked egg, mashed
2 tablespoons chili sauce
3 drops Worcestershire sauce
dash salt and pepper
mayonnaise

Combine all ingredients in small bowl, add enough mayonnaise to moisten. Serve on bed of lettuce with crackers.

TACO DIP
from Barb Bell aboard "Gypsy"

1 (8 ounce) package cream cheese, room temperature
½ pound Cheddar cheese, grated
lettuce, chopped (3-4 cups)
2 tomatoes, diced
taco sauce to cover

Spread cream cheese over plate, cover with lettuce, tomatoes, cheese and taco sauce. Serve with Doritos or Tostados.

Beverages

COFFEE COCOA

1 heaping teaspoon instant coffee
1 heaping teaspoon sweet cocoa
sprinkle of ground cinnamon
1 cup water

Bring water to a boil. Place ingredients in cup and pour water in, let brew for 1 minute then sip slowly.

SWISS MOCHA

1 teaspoon sweet cocoa
1 teaspoon instant coffee
1 teaspoon dry milk
1 tablespoon honey
1 cup water

Bring water to boil. Place ingredients in a cup and pour boiled water over, let sit 1 minute and drink.

CAFÉ VANILLA

1 cup water
1 teaspoon instant coffee
½ teaspoon vanilla extract
1 teaspoon sugar or honey

Bring water to a boil. Place ingredients into cup, pour on boiled water and drink.

HOT LEMON DRINK

½ fresh lemon
1 cup boiling water

Mix above ingredients in cup. Let sit 1 minute and drink.

CRANBERRY HOT TEA

3 cups boiling water
3 tea bags
1½ cups cranberry juice
¼ cup brown sugar or honey

In small saucepan bring water to boil and add tea bags. Let steep for 5 minutes. Remove tea bags, stir in remaining ingredients. Heat until honey or sugar dissolves. Serve.

SUN TEA

1 quart cold water
4 tea bags

In a glass quart container fill with water and place tea bags in. Close lid and place in sun for about 3-4 hours.

CINNAMON COFFEE OR TEA

When making your favorite drip coffee in a pot before adding your boiling water, sprinkle in a small amount of cinnamon powder. If you are making coffee or tea by the cup, place a small stick of cinnamon in the cup. Drink up its delicious.

❍❍❍❍❍❍❍❍❍❍❍❍❍❍❍❍❍❍❍❍❍❍❍❍❍❍❍❍❍❍❍❍❍❍❍❍❍

INSTANT RUSSIAN TEA
from Freda Clary aboard "Clary O"

2 cups Tang
1 cup sugar
½ cup instant tea
3 ounces lemon twist (or any lemonade powder)
½ teaspoon ground cinnamon
½ teaspoon ground cloves

Mix together. Store in airtight container. Use 2 teaspoons to one cup of hot water.

HOT TOMATO JUICE

1 small can tomato juice
½ teaspoon celery salt
¼ teaspoon garlic powder
¼ teaspoon basil
1 tablespoon lemon juice
¼ teaspoon hot sauce

Combine all ingredients and bring to a boil, reduce heat and simmer for 2 minutes. Serve and sip slowly.

COFFEE ANISETTE

1 cup hot black coffee
1 jigger anisette

Make a cup of coffee, pour in jigger of anisette, stir lightly. Sip slowly. Enjoy.

ooo

ORANGE MIMOSA

1 bottle of white champagne
1 large container orange juice

Chill both ingredients, and in a champagne glass fill half of orange juice and half of champagne. Toast and drink slowly.

WINE AND CHAMPAGNE PUNCH

1 large bottle white wine
2 bottles white champagne
1 large bottle of Sprite or Slice
1 cup crushed strawberries (optional)

Chill wine, champagne and soda. Mix in large bowl, and top with favorite slice of fruit or strawberries.

COOL RASPBERRY DRINK

from Linda Mailhot aboard ''Lentetee''

3½ cups mashed raspberry
6 ounces orange juice
2 bottles sparkling wine

Chill, mix and serve.

RUM AND APPLE JUICE

1½ jiggers of rum
1 glass of apple juice, chilled

Mix above ingredients and sip slowly.

SANGRIA PUNCH

1 bottle dry red wine
1 (7 ounce) bottle club soda
juice of whole lemon
2 tablespoons sugar
1 peach, sliced
1 lemon, sliced thin

Put about a dozen ice cubes in a large pitcher. Add lemon juice, sugar, and sliced fruit. Add wine, club soda and stir. Serve.

GRAND MARNIER
from Warren Coleman aboard "Cop Out"

1 cup sugar
½ cup water
3 cups brandy (inexpensive)
2 teaspoons pure orange extract

Mix sugar and water together heat 3 minutes, stirring. Let cool. Add brandy, orange extract, stirring. Place in tight lidded bottle shaking everyday for 3 weeks. Then drink.

HOT BUTTERED RUM

1 cup boiling water
1 jigger rum
1 pat butter
½ teaspoon brown sugar

Place ingredients into cup, pour boiling water on top. Drink slowly.

Breads,
Biscuits,
Buns

CRANBERRY NUT BREAD

2 cups all purpose flour
1 cup honey
1½ teaspoons baking powder
½ teaspoon baking soda
1 teaspoon salt
¼ cup shortening
¾ cup orange juice
1 tablespoon grated orange rind
1 egg, beaten
½ cup chopped nuts
1 cup fresh cranberries, halved and uncooked

In a large bowl, sift together flour, sugar, baking powder, baking soda and salt. Add shortening and blend until mixture resembles coarse cornmeal. In a small bowl combine orange juice, grated rind, with beaten egg. Pour the liquid into the dry ingredients and mix just enough to dampen. Don't beat. Fold in nuts and berries. Grease one large baking pan or two loaf pans. Line pans with wax paper and place mixture into pan. Bake at 350° for 35-40 minutes or until dry test with toothpick. Remove from oven, turn cakes onto wire rack, remove wax paper and let cool.

WALNUT BREAD

from Mary Ellen Williams aboard "Cavu"

3 cups all purpose flour
1 cup sugar
4 teaspoons baking powder
1 teaspoon salt
¾ cup shortening
1 cup chopped walnuts
1 egg, beaten
1½ cups milk
1 teaspoon vanilla

Mix flour, sugar, baking powder and salt in large bowl. Cut in shortening. Stir ¾ cup walnuts. Add egg, milk and vanilla. Mix until ingredients are blended. Pour into greased floured loaf pan and sprinkle remaining walnuts over top. Bake 350° for 50-60 minutes or until loaf is brown. Let stand in pan 10 minutes then turn onto wire rack to cool.

QUICK GINGERBREAD

1½ cups all purpose flour
1 teaspoon ginger
1 teaspoon baking powder
¾ cup water
¼ cup oil
¼ cup honey
raisins and chopped nuts (optional)

Mix all ingredients well in medium bowl. Pour into greased loaf pan. Bake 375° 20-30 minutes.

●●

SCOTCH SHORTBREAD
from Mary Thomson aboard "Ringers Rival"

½ pound margarine or butter
½ cup sugar
2½ cups flour
pinch of salt

Cream margarine or butter with sugar. Add flour, salt, mix well. Press in ungreased pan and bake 350° for 30 minutes or until lightly brown.

RICH EGG BREAD

6 tablespoons shortening
2 cups warm water
2 tablespoons sugar
3 teaspoons salt
2 packages dry active yeast
3 eggs, slightly beaten (hold out one egg yolk for glazing)
6-7 cups unbleached flour

Place shortening, water, sugar, salt, and eggs in large mixing bowl. In another bowl place two cups flour, yeast and mix together. Place this mixture into liquids and beat for 2 minutes. Gradually add the remaining flour. Turn out on floured board, knead for 5 minutes. Replace dough in oiled bowl, cover and let rise in warm place until doubled. Divide into 2 large or 3 small loaves, place in greased loaf pans and let rise again. Brush top with following mixture of egg yolk, 2 tablespoons water. Bake 400° for 35-40 minutes or until golden brown. Remove from pans immediately onto wire racks. Cool before slicing.

INDIAN FRY BREAD
from Thelma Holt aboard "Maggie Duff"

3 cups self rising flour
½ cup lard or solid vegetable shortening
1 cup warm water
vegetable oil

Combine flour and shortening, add water. Mix well, to smooth satin ball. Spread vegetable oil over dough, cover bowl with towel, let rest 30 minutes. Pinch off dough about size of golf ball, pat, flatten, shaping into large circle it should be very thin. Fry in hot vegetable oil on both sides, drain. Serve with honey or eat as is.

PUMPKIN BREAD

½ cup plus 2 tablespoons butter
3 cups all purpose flour
2 teaspoons baking soda
½ teaspoon baking powder
1 teaspoon cinnamon
1 teaspoon ground cloves
1 teaspoon salt
2½ cups sugar
4 eggs
2 cups canned pumpkin
½ cup chopped nuts
½ cup raisins

Place flour, baking soda, baking powder, cinnamon, cloves, salt and sugar in large bowl. In a small bowl cream butter and sugar. Add eggs, then stir in pumpkin, add to flour mixture. When well blended, add nuts and raisins. Grease two loaf pans and bake 350° 40-50 minutes turn over onto wire racks to cool before slicing.

PRESSURE COOKER BREAD "GYPSY"

from Barb Bell aboard "Gypsy"

4 cups flour
1½ cups water (warm)
2 teaspoons salt
1 tablespoon sugar
2 envelopes of dry yeast

Dissolve yeast, sugar and salt in warm water. Add flour, 1 cup at a time. When all flour is in start kneading with your hands until dough is elastic and no longer sticks to your hands. cover bowl with a towel and put in warm place for 1 hour. Dough should be doubled in size. Punch down. Grease pressure cooker (6 quart) with solid shortening. Coat pot with corn meal. (This acts as an insulating barrier so bread cooks evenly.) Place dough in cooker, rise again (45 minutes) place lid on pressure cooker, LEAVE OFF STEAM VALVE . . . COOK OVER LOW FLAME FOR 40 MINUTES. USE FLAME TAMER SO IT DOESN'T BURN. Then check sides and bottom for brownness. Top will not brown but you can flip the bread over and bake another 15-20 minutes.

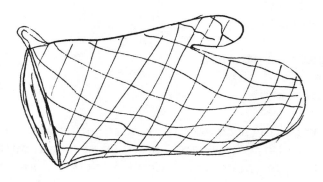

CORN BREAD ANN EVANS
from Miriam Field aboard "Camelot"

1 cup yellow corn meal
1 cup sour cream
1 can cream style corn
2 eggs
1½ teaspoons salt
2 teaspoons baking powder
½ cup corn oil

Mix all ingredients in large bowl. Pour into pan or iron skillet. Bake in oven 350° for 30-40 minutes. Serves 8.

SALT WATER BREAD
from Susan Uhlman aboard "Unknown"

1½ cups sea water
1 tablespoon sugar
1 tablespoon yeast, melted in warm sea water
4 cups flour

Combine all above ingredients and stir well. No kneading necessary. Grease and flour pressure cooker (without valve) or heavy pan. Put dough in cooker with lid on and let rise in warm place for 2 hours. Then cook on low flame on top of stove for ½ hour. Turn loaf over and cook on other side additional 15 minutes. Let cool before slicing.

BEER BREAD SHADOWFAX
from Mary Carol Jones aboard "Shadowfax"

3 cups flour (plain)
2 tablespoons sugar
1 can beer (12 ounces) room temperature
½ stick butter or margarine
pre-heat oven to 350°

Combine flour, sugar and beer in small bowl and mix. Melt butter in loaf pan and pour bread batter directly on top of butter. Bake at 350° for 1 hour or until golden brown. Delicious crunchy, loaf of fresh bread. Can also be baked on top of stove in a Dutch oven or pressure cooker.

BUTTERMILK BREAD

2 cups buttermilk (buttermilk powder comes in cans)
1 teaspoon salt
4 cups self rising flour
1 tablespoon poppy or caraway seed
½ cup raisins

In large bowl mix the above ingredients and pour into a well greased loaf pan. This batter is a sticky one. Bake 350° for 1 hour, cool before slicing.

SPOON BREAD

2 cups buttermilk
1 cup yellow corn meal
1 cup boiling water
dash of salt
2 eggs, beaten
1 tablespoon butter
1 teaspoon baking soda

In a medium saucepan bring water to a boil. Add corn meal and butter, stir until smooth. Take off stove, add baking soda, salt, buttermilk and eggs. Beat well and pour into greased baking pan. Bake about 30-40 minutes. Serve warm.

DATE NUT BREAD

1 cup chopped nuts
1 cup chopped dates
1 teaspoon baking soda
1 cup boiling water
1 tablespoon butter
¾ cup brown sugar
pinch of salt
1 egg
1⅓ cups all purpose flour
1 teaspoon vanilla

Mix all ingredients well, pour into lightly greased loaf pan. Bake 350° 1 hour.

CARAWAY BEER BREAD

3 cups self rising flour
1 (12 ounce) can of beer, room temperature
3 tablespoons sugar
1 tablespoon caraway seeds

Mix together the above ingredients and put into greased loaf pan. Bake 350° for 1 hour. Spread melted butter on top when it comes out of oven. Let cool before slicing.

WHOLE WHEAT RAISIN BREAD

1 cup whole wheat flour
3 teaspoons baking powder
1 teaspoon salt
2 tablespoons powder milk
1 cup wheat germ
¼ cup honey
¾ cup milk
2 tablespoons vegetable oil
2 eggs, beaten
½ cup raisins

Mix first four ingredients in a bowl. Add the remaining ingredients. Grease loaf pan. Bake at 350° for 15-20 minutes or until golden brown.

LAZY LAURA'S BREAD
from Laura Bristol aboard "Hope"

1 tablespoon yeast
2 tablespoons honey or sugar
1 cup powder milk
¼ cup oil
whole wheat flour
unbleached white flour
(see recipe directions below for amounts of flour)

Fill a bowl (about the same size as your pressure cooker) ¼ -
⅓ full of warm water. Add yeast, honey or sugar, milk, oil and
enough whole wheat flour to make it look like cake batter. If
you want variations, add a little oatmeal or bran, soaked wheat
berries, or wheat germ. Cover and let sit for as long as you
want. When you get around to it, stir in more flour (white) keep
adding flour until you can knead without it sticking to your
hand. Knead about 5 minutes. Oil bottom and sides of pressure
cooker and sprinkle with corn meal. Plop in dough, cover and
let rise for 1 hour in a warm place. Never put the little cap on,
and don't lock down lid. Cook over lowest flame possible for
about 1½ hours or until you test with a toothpick and it comes
out clean. Top of bread always looks undone until it cools. This
bread has a crunchy crust on bottom and sides. If you like it
softer, let cool in pot with no lid. When cool store in paper bag,
if there's any left.

WHEAT GERM BREAD

1 package active dry yeast
¼ cup warm water
1¼ cups water
¼ cup butter
3 tablespoons honey
2¼ cups all purpose flour
1 cup wheat germ
1 cup whole wheat flour
2 teaspoons salt
1 teaspoon oil
1 tablespoon sesame seeds (optional)

Dissolve yeast in ¼ cup warm water. Let stand for about 2-3 minutes. In small saucepan melt butter in 1¼ cups water. Stir in honey cool mixture. In large bowl place all dry ingredients, then pour in yeast mixture, butter and honey. Blend lightly and turn onto floured surface. Knead about 5 minutes. Cover bowl and place in warm area, let rise 1 hour or double in bulk. Return to floured surface, punch down shape into two loaves or 1 large and place in greased loaf pan. Cover and let rise again for 30 minutes. Bake at 350° for 35 minutes or until browned well.

WHITE BREAD

1 cup milk
1½ cups water
¼ cup butter or margarine
3 tablespoons sugar
1 teaspoon salt
2 packages active dry yeast
7 cups unbleached flour

Combine water, milk, butter in saucepan, heat until liquids are warm. Pour warmed liquids into large bowl. Mix together in separate bowl 2 cups flour, undissolved yeast, sugar, salt. Slowly add this to liquids, beat well. Stir in additional flour to make a soft dough. Turn out on a lightly floured board and knead 5-8 minutes. Place dough in an oiled bowl and cover with wax paper, or towel and let rise in warm place, until doubled about 1 hour. Punch dough down and divide into 3 small loaves or cut in half and have 2 large loaves. Place in loaf pans, cover and let rise again for 1 hour. Bake 400° for 25-30 minutes. Remove from pans and cool on wire rack.

1-2-3 BREAD
from Jean Stakey aboard ''Cat Dancing''

1 can room temperature beer
2 packets of Sweet and Low
3 cups self rising flour

Mix the above ingredients together and place in a greased pan and bake at 350° until done test with toothpick. You can also cook this on top of stove in a heavy panskillet (sprinkle lightly with cornmeal if desired) on moderate heat covered until done. It's easy, try me.

CINNAMON RAISIN BREAD

1 package active dry yeast
1¼ cups warm water
4 tablespoons sugar
2 teaspoons cinnamon
4 cups biscuit mix
⅔ cup golden or dark raisins

Dissolve yeast in water. Add sugar, half of the biscuit mix and beat two minutes, scrape sides and bottom of bowl often. Add remaining biscuit mix, cinnamon and raisins. Blend well, cover and let rise in warm place until double in bulk, 30 minutes. Stir down batter and beat about 25 strokes. Spread batter in greased loaf pan, cover again and let rise until batter reaches ½ inch from top of pan, 30 minutes. Bake at 375° 45 minutes, or until well browned. Remove from pan, cool on wire rack before slicing.

BEER BREAD

3 cups self rising flour
2 tablespoons honey
1 can (8 ounce) warm beer
¼ cup butter, melted

Mix together flour, honey and beer. Spread in greased loaf pan. Gently pour melted butter over dough. Bake 350° for 1 hour.

SPINNAKER BREAD

from Karen Upham aboard ''Loblolly''

2 packages yeast
2¼ cups warm water
¾ cup non fat dry milk
2 teaspoons salt
3 tablespoons oil
6½ cups flour

Dissolve yeast in water. Stir in milk, salt, oil, gradually adding flour last. Knead 10 minutes. Let rest 20 minutes. Place dough in greased bread tins. I use the small ones. Cover with plastic wrap and place in refrigerator 2-6 hours. Take out of refrigerator and let stand 10 minutes at room temperature. Bake in heavy pot (pressure cooker with vent off), on a rack for 30-40 minutes. Let cool before slicing.

OATMEAL HONEY BREAD

1 cup rolled oats, regular
2 cups boiling water
2 packages active dry yeast
⅓ cup warm water
½ cup honey
¼ cup oil
½ cup powdered milk
6-7 cups whole wheat flour
2 teaspoons salt

Dissolve yeast in warm water and let stand 5 minutes. In large bowl place oats and boiling water, let stand until warm. Add honey, oil and dry ingredients. Knead well for 5 minutes. Let rise in covered bowl until double in bulk. Shape into two loaves. Let rise for 15 minutes and bake in greased loaf pans at 325° for 1 hour.

●○●

COCONUT BREAD

from Norma Henderson aboard "Cera"

4 cups flour
2 teaspoons sugar
1 package dry yeast
1 teaspoon salt
1½ cups coconut cream

Coconut cream is made by grating the meat from a coconut, putting the meat in a muslin bag and squeeze and squeeze. You should get enough cream for your bread from one nut. Put all the dry ingredients into a large bowl (warmed) pour in coconut cream. Knead until the dough is smooth, pliable and elastic. Cover the bowl with damp cloth and leave in a warm place to rise. When doubled in size punch down, shape and put into warm bread tin until well risen and bake in hot oven for 45 minutes.

FANNY'S LOAF

1 stick of butter
2 packages active yeast
2 cups warm water
4 cups flour
1 tablespoon salt
½ cup sugar or honey
½ cup evaporated milk

Mix yeast and warm water, stir until completely dissolved. Add flour and mix. Add additional flour if necessary. Knead for 5 minutes. Shape into ball and place back in bowl, cover and let rise in warm place about 1½ hours or double in bulk. Punch down, and let rise again about ½ hour. Shape into 2 large or 3 small loaves. Place in greased tins, cover and let rise again about 30 minutes. Bake 375° for 35-45 minutes. Place on wire racks to cool.

HOME MADE BISCUIT MIX

1 cup shortening
4½ cups all purpose flour
½ tablespoon salt
2 tablespoons baking powder

Make your own biscuit mix. Mix above ingredients and store in tightly covered container.

ENGLISH MUFFINS ALA RUTH
from Ruth Kates aboard the "Ruth K"

2 cups all purpose flour
1 package active dry yeast
1 cup whole wheat flour
½ cup wheat germ
½ cup uncooked oats
1 cup dry milk powder
2 teaspoons salt
2 cups warm water
¼ cup oil

Place first seven ingredients into a large mixing bowl. Then add warm water and oil, beat in with spoon add gradually more white flour about 2 cups to make a firm dough. Knead 8 minutes. Let rise until double. Knead again and shape into flat ½" thick muffins. Let rise. Bake in oiled skillet (medium heat) till brown on each side. Remove and let cool. When ready to toast, split and toast under grill or split and brown in skillet in a bit of butter. Enjoy.

HOT CEREAL CINNAMON MUFFINS

1¼ cups uncooked instant hot cereal
½ cup apple juice
2 tablespoons oil
¼ cup honey
1 egg
1 cup yogurt or buttermilk
1¼ cups whole wheat flour
1 teaspoon baking soda
½ teaspoon cinnamon
½ cup raisins
½ cup chopped nuts (optional)

In large bowl, combine the cereal and apple juice, blend well. Add oil, honey, egg, buttermilk or yogurt. Add flour, baking soda, cinnamon to cereal mixture. Stir lightly. Then add raisins and chopped nuts. Pour batter into greased muffin tins. Bake 375° 12-15 minutes.

BROWN SUGAR MUFFINS

2 cups all purpose flour
1 teaspoon baking soda
¼ teaspoon salt
1 cup packed light brown sugar
1 egg
1 cup milk
½ cup butter

Mix flour, baking soda, salt and sugar in medium bowl. In separate bowl, beat egg, milk and butter then add all at once to flour mixture. Beat another 5 minutes. Spoon into 12 muffin tins. Bake 350° 20 minutes or until golden brown.

WHEAT GERM MUFFINS ALA JILL

1 egg, well beaten
⅓ cup raw sugar
1¼ cups milk
⅓ cup melted butter
1 cup unbleached white flour or ½ cup unbleached
  flour + ½ cup whole wheat flour
½ teaspoon salt
4 teaspoons baking powder
1 cup wheat germ

Beat together egg, sugar, milk, and butter. Sift together flour, salt, baking powder and mix into the egg mixture. Stir in wheat germ lightly. Fill muffin cups ⅔ full and bake 425° for 20 minutes. Serve with butter or your favorite jam.

BLUEBERRY LEMON MUFFINS

1 cup blueberries (fresh)
1 teaspoon grated lemon peel
2 tablespoons honey
1¾ cups all purpose flour
½ cup sugar
2½ teaspoons baking powder
¼ teaspoon salt
¾ cup milk
⅓ cup oil
1 egg, beaten

Mix blueberries, lemon, honey and set aside. Combine flour, sugar, baking powder and salt. Beat egg, milk and oil, stir into flour mixture lightly. Fold in blueberry mixture. Fill greased muffin tins. Bake 375° for 20-25 minutes.

ZUCCHINI MUFFINS

2 cups whole wheat flour
3 teaspoons baking powder
1 teaspoon cinnamon
¼ teaspoon salt
2 eggs
¾ cup milk
⅓ cup oil
¼ cup honey
1 cup zucchini, grated
¼ cup chopped nuts and raisins (optional)

In a large bowl beat eggs, milk, oil and honey. Then add dry ingredients and stir lightly. Add zucchini, place in greased muffin tins. Bake 350° 12-15 minutes or until golden brown.

JUST PLAIN BISCUITS

⅓ cup shortening
2 cups all purpose flour
2½ teaspoons baking powder
1 teaspoon salt
⅔ cup milk

Cut shortening into flour, baking powder and salt. Stir in milk so dough leaves side of bowl. Turn dough onto floured surface and knead lightly for 2-3 minutes. Roll or pat dough into ½″ thickness. Cut dough into 12 biscuit shapes and place on ungreased cookie sheet. Bake at 400° for 10-12 minutes.

TEA SCONES

from Helen Owen aboard ''Hel's Belles III''

2 cups flour
2 teaspoons sugar
2½ teaspoons baking powder
½ teaspoon salt
⅓ cup milk
⅓ cup shortening
2 eggs (save white from one egg)
handful of raisins

Save some egg white to coat top of scone before baking. Sift dry ingredients. Mix eggs and milk. Cut shortening into dry ingredients. Add raisins then eggs, milk all at once. Roll on floured board mix with fork. Cut dough into triangles, place on greased cookie sheet. Cover with egg white. Bake at 450° for 12 minutes.

QUICK CORN FRITTERS

1 medium can cream style corn
2 eggs
¼ teaspoon salt
2 tablespoons flour
2 tablespoons butter, melted
1 tablespoon honey

Mix the above ingredients. Drop by spoon into skillet with about 1 ″ of cooking oil. Fry on both sides.

⊙⊙

RAISIN SCONES

2⅓ cups Bisquick mix
3 tablespoons honey or sugar
¾ cup raisins
1 egg, beaten
½ cup milk
milk and sugar for topping

In mixing bowl beat egg and milk, add sugar, or honey and raisins, stir lightly. Add Bisquick and blend thoroughly. Place mixture on floured board and work into ½" thick strip. Make diagonal cuts with knife, brush with milk and sprinkle with sugar. Bake on greased cookie sheet 375° for 10-12 minutes. Makes ½ dozen.

EASY BAGELS

2½ - 3 cups all purpose flour
1¼ cups whole wheat flour
2 packages active dry yeast
1½ cups warm water
3 tablespoons honey
2 teaspoons salt

In large mixing bowl place 1 cup of flour and yeast. In separate bowl mix honey, water and salt then add to flour mixture. Beat until well blended. Stir in remaining flours. Knead 10-12 minutes. Cut dough into small portions to form shape of bagel. Cover and let rise for 15-20 minutes. In a very large pot boil water and add honey. Put 3-4 bagels into water and boil for 5-7 minutes, turn once and boil additional 3 minutes. Place boiled bagels on a greased cookie sheet. Bake 375° 25-35 minutes. (Optional make an egg yolk glaze with your favorite sesame, caraway, or poppy seed, brush top of bagels before baking.

Breakfast

●○

SAUSAGE, EGG, CHEESE CASSEROLE
from Lucille Strubell aboard "Kool Kat"

Make night before and let set in refrigerator.
1 pound sausage — mild or hot to your taste
6 slices bread
8 ounces Cheddar cheese (shredded)
6 eggs, beaten
2 cups milk
1 teaspoon dry mustard
1 teaspoon salt
Pepper to taste

Fry sausage till done, drain on paper towels until cool. Tear bread into chunks and place on bottom of greased 9″ x 13″ pan. Spread cool sausage on bread. Sprinkle Cheddar cheese over sausage. In a separate bowl mix together eggs, milk, mustard, salt and pepper. Pour gently over bread, sausage and cheese. Cover casserole and put in cool place overnight. Put in cold oven. Bake 350° 45 minutes. Serves 5. Serve with mixed fruit.

EGGS BENEDICT

4 English muffins
8 pieces cooked ham, thin slices
4 eggs, poached
pepper
Hollandaise sauce (see page 186)

Split English muffins and toast. Place a piece of cooked ham on top, then a poached egg. Pour Hollandaise sauce on top. Serves 2-4.

●○●

WHOLE WHEAT PANCAKES
from Rebecca Horne aboard "Trilani"

1¼ cups whole wheat flour
2 tablespoons sugar
2 teaspoons baking powder
2 tablespoons oil
1⅓ - 1½ cups water or ½ cup milk + ¾ to one cup water
  (Batter should be thin enough to pour.)

Make a hole in the center of the dry ingredients. Pour liquid in and mix with a wooden spoon until ingredients are blended. The batter should be somewhat lumpy, which makes the cakes light. If you beat the batter smooth, the pancakes will be tough. You can replace ¼ cup flour with ¼ cup corn meal when mixing dry ingredients. Heat griddle over a medium high flame, it's hot enough when water dropped on griddle turns to beads. Oil slightly, pour cakes and flip them when tops bubble.

VARIATION: Add 1 cup Tofu, well mashed to batter for a heavier, moist pancake. Serves 3-4.

SAVORY EGGS

1 medium onion, diced
4 eggs
½ teaspoon salt
2 tablespoons water
dash of pepper

Place onion in small amount of butter and sauté. Beat remaining ingredients and add to onions, scramble eggs. Serves 2.

EGG IN THE NEST

1 slice of bread (cut out small hole in center of slice, save this piece)
1 tablespoon butter
1 egg
dash salt and pepper

Melt butter in pan, place bread and small cut out piece in pan. Crack egg open and place into hole of bread. Fry 2 minutes, turn and do the other side. Serve.

HOME MADE GRANOLA

4 cups uncooked regular rolled oats
¼ cup honey
½ cup oil
pinch of salt
1 teaspoon vanilla
½ cup wheat germ
1 cup shredded coconut
¼ cup sesame seeds
1 cup chopped nuts (your choice)

Mix together all dry ingredients in large bowl. Add honey, oil, and vanilla and coat well. Spread on a cookie sheet and bake at 350° 30-40 minutes or until lightly browned and crisp. Cool, store in covered container. Makes about 2 quarts.

WESTERN OMELET

4 eggs
¼ cup water
1 green pepper, medium, diced
1 onion, medium, diced
¼ cup ham, diced
3 tablespoons butter
dash of seasoned salt
dash of pepper
dash of basil
dash of oregano

In skillet melt butter, sauté onions and green pepper. Place eggs, water, seasonings in mixing bowl and beat well. Pour egg mixture over sautéing ingredients and as eggs cook keep pushing cooked portion toward center of skillet. When all loose egg is firm, fold in half and cook additional 2 minutes. Serves 3.

SAILORS CORN SCRAMBLE
from Helen Dodson aboard "Terrapin"

4-6 strips of bacon (per person)
1 small can kernel corn
3 eggs, slightly beaten
pepper and salt to taste

Fry bacon, remove. Heat corn in bacon fat. Stir in eggs and stir gently until cooked thoroughly. Serve and surround with bacon. Serves 2

⬬⬬⬬⬬⬬⬬⬬⬬⬬⬬⬬⬬⬬⬬⬬⬬⬬⬬⬬⬬⬬⬬⬬⬬⬬⬬⬬⬬⬬⬬⬬⬬⬬⬬⬬⬬⬬⬬⬬

TACO OMELET

from Becky Aldrich aboard "Nel Fenwick"

3 eggs, beaten
1 small onion, chopped
2 tablespoons taco sauce
½ cup grated cheese (your favorite)
2 tablespoons olives, chopped
1 small green pepper, diced

Mix eggs in bowl, pour into buttered skillet and sprinkle in the remaining ingredients. As soon as eggs set fold over top and cook 2 minutes longer and serve. Serves 2.

WELSH GRIDDLE CAKES

from Angela Wellman aboard "Suffolk Punch"

1 cup self rising flour
½ teaspoon salt
3 ounces shortening
3 ounces sugar
2 ounces currants
½ teaspoon nutmeg or cinnamon
1 egg
2 tablespoons milk

Mix flour, and salt in a bowl. With a fork work in shortening. Add sugar, currants and spice. Mix to a fairly stiff dough with egg and milk. Roll out on a floured board until ¼" thick, cut into rounds with a 2" cutter. Bake in a well-greased, heavy frying pan or griddle, moderately hot, for 3 minutes on each side. Serve hot or cold. Good sprinkled with sugar or buttered. Serves 2.

NOVA SCOTIA PANCAKES
from Joan Smith aboard "Atria"

Combine:
1½ cups of flour
2 teaspoons baking powder
½ teaspoon salt
Mix:
1⅔ cups milk
Then add:
2 egg yolks (save the whites)
2 tablespoons butter

In separate bowl, beat 2 egg whites stiff but not dry. Fold into flour mixture, adding more milk if necessary for pancake consistency. Drop pancake batter by spoonfuls on lightly greased frying pan or griddle. Cook until bubbles appear, then turn and cook until browned. Serves 2 "piggies" or 3 normal people!

PEANUT BUTTER FRENCH TOAST
from Helen Caesar aboard "Mal de Terre"

Make a peanut butter sandwich, dip in beaten egg and fry . . . top with hot apple sauce . . . easy to do.

ooo

HOT COOKED OATMEAL

1½ cups old fashioned oats
2 cups water
pinch of salt
butter dot
brown sugar (sprinkle)

Bring salt and water to a boil, add oats and cover. Cook on low flame for 2 minutes. Remove from heat and let sit while you prepare the serving bowls. In each individual bowl add dot of butter, brown sugar and pour in cooked oatmeal. It's great to eat on those chilly mornings. Serves 2.

SCRAMBLED EGGS & CHEESE

2 eggs
1 tablespoon butter
¼ teaspoon Worcestershire sauce
dash of salt and pepper
¼ cup grated cheese (Swiss or Cheddar)

In a small bowl mix eggs, sauce and seasonings. In hot skillet melt butter and pour in egg mixture. Sprinkle cheese on top, mix slowly until set. Serves 2.

Salads,
Sandwiches,
Soups

AMBROSIA SALAD
from Marcie Cragg aboard "Marcie"

1 can mandarin oranges, drained
1 can crushed pineapple, drained
½ bag shredded coconut
½ or whole bag (10 ounces) miniature marshmallows
   depending on your love of them
1 cup sour cream

Combine and store overnight in the refrigerator. Serve cold.

AVOCADO CHEESE SALAD

1 avocado, peeled and sliced
2 medium tomatoes, chopped
1 medium onion, sliced
1 cup shredded cheese, your favorite
1 tablespoon chili powder
¼ teaspoon salt
¼ teaspoon basil
¼ cup oil
¼ cup apple cider vinegar
dash pepper

In large bowl place cheese, avocado, tomatoes, and onion. In separate bowl add remaining ingredients, mix well, pour over veggies and serve.

FRUIT SALAD

4 oranges, sliced
4 bananas, sliced
2 large apples, sliced
1 small can crushed pineapple (drain juice in small
  saucepan)
1 cup chopped walnuts
1 cup chopped dates
1 cup seedless grapes
1 cup marshmallows
1 tablespoon honey

Dressing:
1 cup sugar
1 teaspoon flour
1 egg, beaten
dash of salt
juice from pineapple
1 tablespoon lemon juice

Prepare Dressing: In a small bowl beat egg with 1 tablespoon
water. Place lemon and pineapple juice into saucepan and heat
on low flame, then add egg mixture. Blend in remaining ingredients, remove from heat, let cool before placing dressing
on fruit.

WALDORF SALAD

3-4 apples (cut in bite-size pieces)
½ cup celery, sliced
½ cup chopped nuts
½ cup mayonnaise
1 tablespoon honey
1 tablespoon lemon juice
⅛ teaspoon salt

In small bowl mix mayonnaise, honey, lemon juice and salt. Add apples, celery and nuts, toss lightly. Serve.

FIVE BEAN SALAD

1 can green beans
1 can wax beans
1 can lima beans
1 can red kidney beans
1 can garbanzo beans
½ cup water
¾ cup wine vinegar
2 tablespoons honey
¼ teaspoon basil
2 cloves garlic, minced

In a large mixing bowl place water, vinegar, honey, basil and garlic stir well. Drain all beans, place in bowl, let marinate about 1 hour.

FOUR BEAN SALAD

1 pound can cut green beans
1 pound can cut wax yellow beans
1 pound can lima beans
1 pound can red kidney beans
1 medium green pepper, chopped
1 medium green onion, thinly sliced

Marinade:
½ cup sugar
½ teaspoon dried tarragon
½ cup wine vinegar
½ cup salad oil
1 teaspoon salt
½ teaspoon dry mustard
½ teaspoon basil
2 tablespoons snipped parsley
2 teaspoons oregano

Drain beans. In large bowl, add green pepper and onion to beans. Mix marinade separately, then add to bean mixture. Toss carefully. Cover and refrigerate overnight. The longer it sits the better it is.

GREEN PEA SALAD
from Cozy May aboard "Cat's Meow"

1 (17 ounce) can early peas
3 hard boiled eggs, chopped
½ cup sweet pickle, chopped
1 small jar pimiento, cut in small pieces
⅓ teaspoon celery seed
¼ cup mayonnaise

Combine ingredients, mix well, chill and serve.

CORN SALAD MARINATED
from Angela Wellman aboard "Suffolk Punch"

1 (19 ounce) can whole kernel corn, drained
1 medium onion, thinly sliced
½ cup celery, diced
½ cup carrot, shredded

Dressing:
⅔ cup salad oil
3 tablespoons white vinegar
2 tablespoons lemon juice
½ teaspoon oregano
¼ teaspoon curry powder
¼ teaspoon garlic
⅛ teaspoon pepper

Shake dressing ingredients in a closed jar. Pour over salad and mix well. Leave for about 4 hours to marinate before serving.

SPROUT SALAD

2 cups mixed sprouts fresh or 1 can bean sprouts, drained
1 can water chestnuts, cut in half
2 tablespoons honey
3 tablespoons vinegar
2 tablespoons oil
1 tablespoon lemon juice
dash salt and pepper
dash basil
dash thyme
dash oregano

Combine all ingredients in bowl, toss lightly and serve.

PICKLED GARDEN RELISH

½ cauliflower, cut into flowerettes
2 carrots, cut into 2″ strips
2 stalks celery, cut into 1″ strips
1 green pepper, cut into 2″ strips
1 jar (4 ounce) pimiento, drained, cut into small pieces
1 jar (3 ounce) green olives, drained
¾ cup wine vinegar
½ cup olive or salad oil
2 tablespoons sugar or honey
½ teaspoon oregano
¼ teaspoon black pepper

In large skillet combine ingredients with ¼ cup water bring to boil, stir occasionally, reduce heat, simmer for 5 minutes covered. Cool then place mixture into containers and refrigerate. Serve cold.

FRESH TOMATO-BASIL SALAD

6 ripe tomatoes, sliced
3-4 sprigs of scallions, sliced
½ teaspoon salt
½ teaspoon black pepper
¼ cup basil (fresh) or 2 tablespoons basil spice
2 tablespoons vinegar
1/4 cup olive oil

In large bowl place all above ingredients. Toss lightly and serve.

∞∞∞∞∞∞∞∞∞∞∞∞∞∞∞∞∞∞∞∞∞∞∞∞∞∞∞∞∞∞∞∞∞∞∞∞∞∞

CUT CARROT SALAD

from Bonnie McDonald aboard "Bonnie Bird"

2 pounds carrots cut into 1″ cuts or:
3 large cans of carrots
1 large onion, sliced
1 green pepper (cut into thin strips)
1 cup sugar
½ teaspoon pepper
½ cup oil
¾ cup vinegar
1 teaspoon salt
1 teaspoon dry mustard

If using fresh carrots, cook until tender to touch, drain and let cool. In using canned carrots you may select already sliced ones. In large mixing bowl, place carrots, onions and green pepper. In saucepan, bring to boil remaining ingredients and cook until sugar is dissolved. Pour hot mixture over vegetables, refrigerate 8 hours.

FETA CHEESE SALAD

6 medium tomatoes, quartered
3 medium cucumbers, sliced
1 large onion, sliced
6-8 greek olives
1 teaspoon salt
½ cup olive oil
1 teaspoon oregano
1 teaspoon basil
anchovies (optional)

In large bowl place all vegetables. In separate bowl mix thoroughly olive oil, oregano, basil, salt, then add crumbled feta cheese and olives, stir once. Serve over vegetables. Place anchovies on top.

SPAGHETTI SALAD
from Art Silvers aboard ''Echo''

1 pound spaghetti
1 large bottle of Italian dressing
½ jar McCormick Salad Supreme
1 large green pepper, chopped
1 medium chopped onion

Cook spaghetti, drain (do not rinse) add remaining ingredients, mix well. Refrigerate (stir often to marinate). Serves 10, recipe can be cut in half.

CHICK PEA SALAD

3 medium tomatoes, cut into cubes
1 medium cucumber, sliced thin
1 medium green pepper, chopped
2 small onions, diced
3 tablespoons parsley
¼ cup salad oil
2 tablespoons lemon juice
1 tablespoon wine vinegar
1 teaspoon basil
1-2 cloves of minced garlic
½ teaspoon salt
dash of hot pepper
1 can chick peas

Mix all seasonings well. Place fresh vegetables and chick peas in large bowl. Pour seasonings on top. Serve.

FRESH BROCCOLI SALAD

1 bunch of broccoli, cut into bite size pieces
½ cup sliced olives, green or black
1 small can water chestnuts, sliced
1 medium green pepper, thinly sliced
½ cup sliced mushrooms
2 medium tomatoes, sliced in wedges
8 ounces your favorite dressing
croutons (optional)

Combine all ingredients except dressing and mix, then add dressings and toss. Chill 1 hour and top with croutons and serve.

COLD SPAGHETTI SALAD

1 package spaghetti
1 green pepper, diced
1 medium onion, chopped
2-3 stalks celery, diced
1-2 tablespoons chopped pimientos
1 can early peas
mayonnaise to taste

Cook spaghetti, rinse and drain. Cut vegetables and place in large bowl, add spaghetti, add mayonnaise to taste. Chill and serve.

CABBAGE SALAD

from Linda Mailhot aboard ''Lentetee''

1 large cabbage, shredded
4-5 carrots, grated
1 teaspoon salt
1½ cups vinegar
1½ cups oil
½ jar yellow mustard
1 cup sugar

Mix all ingredients and put in a large airtight container. Good for one month or more stored in cool place.

COLD CRAB PIE

1 8-ounce package cream cheese
1 can crabmeat, lightly flaked
1 bottle cocktail sauce

Soften cream cheese, spread in pie tin. Layer flaked crabmeat on cream cheese, and spread cocktail sauce on top. Serve with crackers.

HOT SLAW
from Daniele Gillespie aboard "Kiowa"

1 small head cabbage, chopped
1 medium onion, diced
1 tablespoon salt
3 tablespoons sugar
2 teaspoons mustard
3 tablespoons cooking oil
1 egg
½ cup vinegar
¼ cup water

In saucepan put in the first 5 ingredients stir and cook for 5 minutes. Then add beaten egg, vinegar, water and cook for 20 minutes stirring occasionally, serve.

BREAD AND BUTTER PICKLES

3 large zucchini
4 onions, sliced
2 green peppers, diced
3 tablespoons coarse salt
2 cups vinegar
2 teaspoons turmeric
2 teaspoons celery seed
3 sticks cinnamon or 2 teaspoons of ground cinnamon
1 cup sugar

In large Dutch oven place all ingredients and bring to a boil, then simmer until vegetables are tender. Let cool and store in air tight container.

CRUNCH COLE SLAW
from Lora Wandros aboard "Lora"

1 large head of cabbage, shredded
1 cup sugar
1 green pepper, chopped
1 medium onion, chopped
1 carrot, grated
1 cup cooking oil
1 tablespoon salt
1 cup vinegar, white or cider
1 tablespoon celery seed

In large bowl place cabbage, pepper, onion, celery seed and carrot, toss lightly with sugar. Bring to a boil oil, salt, vinegar, and cool down slightly. Pour over cabbage mixture and stir until well mixed. Store in airtight containers and needs no refrigeration.

CHUTNEY

6 large very ripe tomatoes, chopped
1 green pepper, chopped
1 red pepper, chopped
2 medium onions, chopped
2 tart apples, peeled and chopped
½ cup celery, diced
1-2 cups vinegar
½ teaspoon salt
½ teaspoon cayenne pepper
½ cup sugar

Place all ingredients in large saucepan, cook until thick. Cool down, place in air tight container, refrigerate.

CHICKEN ARTICHOKE SALAD

from Ann Ginsburg aboard "Semper Attempta III"

1 (6 ounce) chicken flavored rice
4 cups diced chicken
2 (6 ounce) jars marinated artichoke hearts,
  undrained
2 green onions, chopped
½ green bell pepper, chopped
slivered almonds (optional)
8 stuffed green olives
½ cup mayonnaise
¼ tablespoon curry powder
salt and pepper to taste

Cook rice as directed. In large bowl, stir cooked rice with fork, let cool. Drain and reserve marinade from artichoke hearts. Add half of reserve marinade to rice and toss. Add artichoke hearts, peppers, olives and toss again. To the remaining artichoke marinade add the mayonnaise, curry powder, salt, pepper and toss lightly. Serve on lettuce with tomato, whole olives and a sprinkle of toasted slivered almonds.

CORNED BEEF SALAD

from Joan Russell aboard "Maerdym"

1 can corned beef
2 hard boiled eggs, mashed
1 medium onion, minced
1 stalk of celery, small pieces
½ bottle of your favorite dressing

Combine all the above ingredients, toss lightly and eat.

ORIENTAL TUNA SALAD
from Alice Allchin aboard "Piwacket"

½ cup canned Chinese veggies, drained
4 ounces water packed tuna, drained
1 tablespoon mayonnaise
½ teaspoon lemon juice
½ teaspoon soy sauce
⅛ - ¼ teaspoon curry powder
1 small onion, diced

Mix tuna, veggies, and onion. Mix mayonnaise, lemon juice, soy sauce and curry powder in a separate bowl. Pour over tuna mix and toss lightly. Better when allowed to stand, chill if possible.

CHICKEN APPLE SALAD

1½ cups chopped cooked chicken
¼ cup celery, chopped
½ cup apples, diced
½ cup green pepper, sliced
¼ cup mayonnaise
2 teaspoons lemon juice
¼ cup chopped nuts (optional)
dash of salt and pepper

Toss all ingredients lightly and serve on bed lettuce.

SPAMWICHES

from Becky Aldrich aboard "Nel Fenwick"

Fry one can of Spam sliced into ⅛" slices. Toast bread (desired amount) with butter and garlic powder. Top garlic toast as follows:
Spam covered with a splash of mustard, onion slices, tomato, cheese, olives, peppers and enjoy.

VEGGIE-PITA QUICK SANDWICH

4 pita shells (cut off about ¼ to have your opening)
2 medium ripe tomatoes, diced
1 medium onion, diced
1 green pepper, diced
1 cucumber, diced
1 cup shredded cabbage
1 cup mixed sprouts
½ cup yogurt dressing
dashes of salt and pepper to taste
1 teaspoon chopped basil

Mix the above ingredients in a bowl. Cut pita bread, stuff with salad. Serve.

FRENCH LOAF SPICY SANDWICH

1 large French loaf
sliced luncheon meats (your favorite)
sliced cheese (Swiss, provolone, etc.)
Olive Salad Topping:
⅔ cup chopped pimiento stuffed green olives
½ cup chopped artichoke hearts
½ teaspoon garlic, minced
3 tablespoons parsley
3 tablespoons olive oil
1 tablespoon tarragon vinegar
dash hot pepper

Mix above all salad topping and set aside. Slice French loaf
bread in half. Scoop out the top portion of bread. On bottom
layer of bread slice, place variety of meats and cheese, top with
olive salad. Close sandwich, place on cookie sheet and bake
350° for 20 minutes or until cheese melts.

QUICK BROWN BREAD SANDWICH

cream cheese
1 can brown bread

Open can of brown bread, slice individual slices of bread.
Spread cream cheese and eat open-face sandwich.

oooooooooooooooooooooooooooooooooooooo

SIMPLE OPEN FACE REUBENS
from Suzanne Stein aboard "Pleiades"

**1 bottle thousand island dressing or your favorite
    kind
1 medium can sauerkraut, drained
1 can corn beef
4-5 slices of your favorite cheese**

Cut several slices of favorite bread to fit bottom of pan, spread
evenly with favorite dressing or thousand island dressing,
cover with sauerkraut. Slice corn beef to lay on top of
sauerkraut, spread with more dressing cover with more
sauerkraut. Bake 375° for 15 minutes then add a topping of
your favorite cheese. Continue baking until cheese is nicely
melted. Serve.

MELTED CHEESE OPEN FACE SANDWICH

**1 cup grated cheese (your favorite)
2 tablespoons milk
2 eggs, beaten
dash cayenne pepper
dash salt
dash basil
toast**

Add cheese to eggs, then add milk and seasoning. Place in
saucepan and cook until thick. Spread on toast.

BACON-LETTUCE-TOMATO SANDWICH

4 strips of bacon (per sandwich)
lettuce
tomato, sliced
mayonnaise
dash pepper
toasted rye bread

Fry bacon, drain on paper towel. Toast bread, spread with mayonnaise. Make a sandwich with ingredients.

REFRIED BEANS IN TACO SHELLS

1 small package taco shells
1 can refried beans
1 cup Cheddar cheese, shredded
2 tablespoons salsa sauce
2 tablespoons oil

Fill each taco shell with some refried beans, salsa sauce and cheese. Heat oil in skillet, place filled tacos in skillet, cover and cook for 3 minutes on each side. Serve.

GRILLED CHEESE & TOMATO SANDWICH

For each sandwich:
1½ slices cheese (Swiss, American, mozzarella)
2 slices tomato
sprinkle with oregano

In skillet melt butter, and place sandwich on top, brown one side then the other till cheese melts. Serve.

APPLE AND PEANUT BUTTER SANDWICH

peanut butter, crunchy or smooth
apples, peeled and sliced thin
honey
your favorite kind of bread

Make a peanut butter sandwich. Before covering, add slices of apple and enough honey to coat the bread.

GRILLED HAM AND CHEESE SANDWICH
¼ pound cooked ham
¼ pound sliced Swiss cheese
tomato slices
2 pats butter

Make a sandwich of ham, cheese and tomato. Using one pat of butter on the sandwich and one pat in the skillet, grill until brown, turn and do flip side.

EGG AND GREEN PEPPER SALAD SANDWICH

6 hard cooked eggs
1 large onion, finely diced
1 large green pepper, diced
mayonnaise
dash of salt and pepper

In medium bowl, mash eggs, add onion, green pepper, salt and pepper. Add enough mayonnaise to make spreadable. Chill before making sandwich.

CREAM CHEESE AND ALFALFA SPROUTS SANDWICH

cream cheese
alfalfa sprouts
tomato, slices
dash salt and pepper
favorite bread

Spread cream cheese on a slice of your favorite bread. Add sprinkles of sprouts, tomato and dashes of salt and pepper. Close sandwich with another slice of bread. Serve.

CHICKEN OR TURKEY SALAD SANDWICH

2 cups leftover chicken or turkey, cut in bite size
  pieces
½ cup celery, diced
1 small onion, diced
dash salt and pepper
mayonnaise

In medium bowl place cut up meat, add remaining ingredients blend well, chill, then make sandwich on your favorite bread or roll.

TUNA FISH SANDWICH

1 can tuna fish
¼ cup celery, diced
1 small onion, diced
1 hard cooked egg, mashed
¼ teaspoon vinegar
dash salt and pepper
½ cup mayonnaise

In bowl break up tuna fish, then add remaining ingredients mix well, and spread on your favorite bread.

PINK SALMON SANDWICH

1 small can salmon
1 hard cooked egg, mashed
1 small onion, diced
½ cup mayonnaise
¼ teaspoon lemon juice
dash salt and pepper

Combine all ingredients in small bowl, mash lightly and spread on your favorite bread.

SHRIMP CURRY SOUP

1 small can shrimp
1 tablespoon flour
2 tablespoons butter
2 cups milk
1 tablespoon parsley
¼ teaspoon curry powder
¼ teaspoon onion salt
dash white pepper

Make a paste of ¼ cup milk and the flour. In a medium saucepan combine remaining ingredients. Cook over medium heat. Add flour paste, stir until thickened. Serve.

ooo

EASY ONION SOUP

3-4 large onions, thinly sliced
¼ cup butter, melted
5 cups boiling water
1 chicken bouillon cube
2 beef bouillon cubes
¼ teaspoon salt
¼ teaspoon white pepper
6 slices French bread, toasted
slice Swiss cheese for each individual bowl

Sauté onion in butter in large pot. Add remaining ingredients except cheese. Bring to a boil and reduce heat, simmer for ½ hour. Pour soup in individual serving bowls, top with bread and sliced cheese. Place under broiler or in oven. When cheese has melted, serve.

FRENCH ONION SOUP

4 tablespoons butter
1 pound onions, thinly sliced
4 cups beef broth
1 cup white wine
4 slices toasted French bread
½ pound Swiss or milk cheese, cut into slices
Parmesan cheese

Melt butter in large 6 quart pot. Add onions and cook slowly, 30 minutes. Add beef broth and simmer 5 minutes. Add wine and simmer another 5 minutes. Pour soup in crockery pots, float 1 piece of toasted bread and cheese on top. Place under broiler until cheese has melted.

SPICY CRAB SOUP

3 quarts water
1 large can V-8 Juice
1 pound can crushed tomatoes
1 pound mixed crabmeat
1 large onion, diced
½ cup celery, diced
1 tablespoon salt
¼ teaspoon black pepper
2 tablespoons Old Bay Seasoning (more to suit taste)
⅛ teaspoon cayenne pepper
1 tablespoon oregano
4 cups mixed fresh vegetables (potatoes, carrots, corn, string beans) cut into bite size pieces. You can substitute fresh vegetables for the following: 1 medium can of each, kernel corn, cut green beans, carrots, potatoes, which you will add to cooked soup the last 10 minutes of cooking.

In a large pot fill with water, juice, tomatoes, seasonings and fresh vegetables, simmer until veggies are tender. Add crabmeat and simmer additional 15 minutes more before serving.

NAVY BEAN SOUP

1 pound navy beans
9 cups water
1 bay leaf
1 teaspoon salt
dash pepper
1 large onion, chopped
2 stalks celery, chopped
2 teaspoons parsley
2-3 cloves garlic, crushed
1 teaspoon oregano
1 teaspoon basil
½ pound neck bones, or ham hock, or necks and
  wings of chicken (your choice)

In large pot soak beans for 1 hour, then bring to boil and add all ingredients, simmer for 1½ hours or until beans are tender. Serve. (If using pressure cooker follow instructions for beans.)

EASY VEGETABLE SOUP

2 carrots, diced
2 Irish potatoes, diced
½ teaspoon salt
¼ teaspoon basil
1 turnip, diced
1 medium onion, chopped
½ teaspoon pepper
1 small can crushed tomatoes
2 - 2½ quarts water

Place all vegetables into water, and simmer for 1 hour. Mash with potato masher and cook additional 5 minutes. Serve.

SHADOWFAX SOUP
from Mary Carol Jones aboard "Shadowfax"

**3 ounces snack ramen oriental noodles (chicken
flavor)
2 cups water
1 egg, beaten
1 scallion, sliced thin
shreds of chicken, crab, or clams (leftovers)**

Boil water, add egg slowly, stirring constantly in water to break
yellow, add leftover shreds of meat and scallions. Cover and
simmer for 3-5 minutes add noodles and continue cooking for
3-5 minutes stirring occasionally. Serve.

HOMEMADE CHICKEN SOUP PLUS

**1 fryer cut in large pieces (including small parts of
chicken not LIVER)
2-3 carrots, peeled and cut
1 large onion, peeled, whole
1-2 stalks celery
1½ quarts cold water
salt and pepper to taste**

Place cut up chicken in cold water in large pot. Add all remaining ingredients and bring to a boil, then drop flame and simmer for 1½ hours. After soup has cooled down, remove chicken.
With hands peel off skin and replace small pieces of loose
chicken back into pot. The larger slices of chicken meat save
to make chicken chow mein, or cold chicken salad. Make some
plain white rice or egg noodles to serve in the soup.

CONCH CHOWDER

from Miriam Field aboard "Camelot"

5-6 large conch
2-3 tablespoons lime juice
1 chopped medium onion
2 carrots, sliced thin
2 good squirts sea water
3 tablespoons bacon fat or 6 slices bacon, cut up
1 can potatoes, sliced
1 can green beans with liquid
1 can zucchini
1 can crushed tomatoes
2 teaspoons chopped parsley
1 medium can V-8 Juice
½ can whole kernel corn
black pepper, Worcestershire sauce, hot sauce to your
   taste

Clean conch, wash, pound flat, soak in water and lime juice
for 1-2 hours. Cut conch in small bite size pieces, add chopped
medium onion, carrots, barely cover with water and simmer
20 minutes (sea water and the rest with fresh). Add bacon,
potatoes, green beans, zucchini, corn, seasonings, juice and
parsley. Simmer additional 10 minutes and serve.

PEANUT BUTTER SOUP

1 quart milk
3 tablespoons peanut butter
dash salt

Place milk in saucepan, just before boiling add salt and peanut
butter. Remove from heat, stir until blended. Serve.

DOC'S CHICKEN SOUP
from Art "Doc" Silvers aboard "Echo"

**Backs, necks, wings, etc. from 2 whole fryers when I
am having fried chicken**
1 quart water
1 large onion, diced
bunch of celery tops
pinch salt and pepper
½ cup instant rice

Place chicken parts in pressure cooker, add water, onion, celery tops, salt and pepper. Bring cooker up to pressure and cook for 20-30 minutes. Set aside and allow to cool (may be left out overnight if you don't open since contents are sterilized). When open skim off excess fat, pick meat, discard skin and bones. Taste and adjust seasoning. Before serving add a little water to give a good solid flavor. Bring to a boil and add ½ cup Minute Rice. Let stand 10 minutes covered before serving.

FISH POTTÉ
from Daniele Gillespie aboard "Kiowa"

5 cups water
1 onion, cut up
1 bay leaf
1 fish (any kind too small for anything else)
1 cup cooked rice and or 1 can mixed vegetables
1 can tomatoes, optional

Cut off the head, scale and clean fish. (Skin can be left on.) Put fish in water with onion and bay leaf. Bring to a boil, cover, cook 15 minutes till fish is done. Remove fish, pick the meat off the bones, and add to the broth, add rice and or vegetables, tomatoes to broth. Heat additional 5 minutes and serve.

QUICK CLAM CHOWDER

3 strips bacon, cut in pieces
1 large diced onion
2-3 carrots, cut in bite size pieces
2 stalks celery
1 small can string beans
½ head cabbage, in bite size pieces
1 small can early peas
1 teaspoon thyme
dash salt and pepper
1 large can whole tomatoes
1 small can potatoes
1 medium size can clams with juice

Place all ingredients into large pot except can peas, string beans and potatoes. Cook on low heat until cabbage is tender, then add remaining ingredients. Cook additional 5-8 minutes and serve.

QUICK OYSTER CHOWDER

2 medium onions, chopped
¼ cup butter
2 tablespoons flour
2 cups potatoes, diced
¼ cup celery, diced
1 teaspoon salt
1 cup water
1 cup milk
1 small can fresh oysters

In medium saucepan sauté onion in butter. Blend in flour slowly. Very slowly add water while stirring. Add potatoes, celery and salt. Cook until potatoes are tender. Add milk and oysters, simmer 7 minutes.

CREAM OF CRAB SOUP

1 pound fresh crabmeat
¼ cup onion, minced
¼ cup butter
2 tablespoons flour
¼ teaspoon celery salt
½ teaspoon salt
¼ teaspoon white pepper
few dashes of Worcestershire sauce
1 cup chicken bouillon
4 cups light cream
2 tablespoons parsley
2 tablespoons sherry for each bowl served (optional)

In Dutch oven pot sauté onion in butter until golden in color. Over medium flame add flour, seasonings stirring constantly. Slowly add the chicken bouillon and cook additional 5 minutes. Add cream, cook slowly until thickened. Next add crabmeat and parsley cook until crabmeat is hot. Serve and add sherry to each individual bowl.

CREAM ASPARAGUS AND MUSHROOM SOUP

from Miriam Field aboard "Camelot"

2 cups white sauce (see page 182)
1 tablespoon instant chicken bouillon
1 medium can asparagus
1 medium can mushrooms

Make 2 cups white sauce, stir in chicken bouillon, add asparagus and mushrooms, grate a little nutmeg, salt and pepper to taste, simmer 2-3 minutes. Serve.

BLACK BEAN SOUP

2 cups black beans
4 cups water
1 green pepper, diced
1 medium onion, diced
2-3 cloves garlic, minced
1 bay leaf
1 cup diced smoke ham
3 strips chopped bacon
salt and pepper to taste

Soak beans for 2 hours. Place beans and same water into pressure cooker. Add remaining ingredients. Cook under pressure for 20 minutes then let pressure drop of own accord. Add smoked ham and simmer for additional 15 minutes. Serve with side dish of diced onion.

One Dish Meals

EGG FOO YOUNG

1 cup cooked chicken or turkey diced
½ cup chopped onion
1 can bean sprouts, drained
3 tablespoons chopped scallions (save for topping)
1 tablespoon soy sauce
¼ teaspoon salt
3 eggs
oil for deep frying
1½ cups chicken bouillon
1 teaspoon molasses
1 teaspoon corn starch, mix with 2 tablespoons water

Place meat, veggies (except scallions), soy sauce, and salt in bowl, mix well together. Break eggs and stir lightly into mixture. Using soup ladle scoop out some mixture and fry in hot oil. Fry until they rise up then turn and fry second side. In separate small saucepan, heat bouillon, molasses, dash of soy sauce, corn starch and water until thick. Serve on top of foo young, sprinkle with scallions.

QUICK SPINACH CASSEROLE

1 package frozen spinach or 1 large can spinach,
   drained
4 tablespoons cottage cheese
1 boiled potato, mashed or ½ cup instant potato
2 eggs, beaten
2 tablespoons diced white cheese
½ teaspoon salt

Combine all ingredients and place in a 1 quart greased casserole. Bake 350° 15 minutes. Serve.

ooo

TUNA OR SALMON TOPSTOVE

from Linda Mailhot aboard "Lentetee"

2 onion, diced
¼ cup butter
1⅓ cups milk
¼ cup flour
1 pound tuna or salmon
½ pound mushrooms, sliced
dash salt and pepper
¼ teaspoon cayenne pepper
2 eggs, beaten
2 tablespoons cream
2 teaspoons lemon juice

Sauté onion in butter. Slowly add milk and blend in flour, cook until thick. Add remaining ingredients, simmer ten minutes. Serve with rice or on toast.

EASY HAMBURGER WITH VEGETABLES

1 pound hamburger
3 carrots, sliced
2-3 potatoes, thinly sliced
1 onion, sliced
3 stalks celery, sliced
salt and pepper to taste
1 (10 ounce) can tomato sauce
1 (10 ounce) can beef consommé

Place layer of hamburger then carrots, potato, onion and celery. In a small bowl mix tomato sauce, beef consommé, salt and pepper, pour onto mixture. Bake 350° 1 hour.

VEGETARIAN LASAGNA

2 large zucchini, cut lengthwise in ¼" slices
¼ cup flour
¾ teaspoon salt
¼ teaspoon pepper
½ cup oil
15 ounces ricotta cheese
2 eggs
1 teaspoon oregano
1 teaspoon basil
4 tablespoons Parmesan cheese
1 medium jar spaghetti sauce
1 package mozzarella cheese, cut into strips

In bowl place zucchini, flour, salt, pepper and toss lightly. In another bowl mix ricotta cheese, eggs, oregano, basil and Parmesan cheese. In a large skillet heat oil and fry zucchini mixture until tender. Then in a large baking dish alternate layers of zucchini mixture, cheese mixture, and sauce. Top with cheese mixture. Bake 350° for 25-30 minutes. Serve.

BEEF AND VEGETABLES
from Linda Mailhot aboard "Lentetee"

1 pound beef chunks, bite size pieces
3 carrots, sliced
2-3 potatoes, sliced
1 onion, sliced
3 stalks celery, cut bite size pieces
1 can (10 ounce) cream of tomato soup
1 can (10 ounce) consommé beef clear soup
dash salt and pepper

Place all ingredients into a small roasting pan, cover and cook in oven 350° for 2 hours or pressure cooker 20 minutes. Let come down on own accord.

STIR FRY 1-2-3

from Pat Brown aboard "Syzygy"

2-3 different kinds of vegetables: green peppers,
  carrots, broccoli, cauliflower, squash, etc. (fresh if
  possible)
beef, pork, shrimp, chicken, or fish (choice of one)
peanuts, shelled

Sauce:
Mix 2 tablespoons corn starch, ¼ cup water, ¼ cup
  sake or white wine, ¼ cup soy sauce

Cut up about 1 cup of each veggie of choice into bite size pieces.
Also cut meat or pork etc. same size. Fry each ingredient about
2 minutes separately in oil. Mix all ingredients together and
place in large dutch oven pour sauce on top, heat until thickened and bubbly, serve.

FRANKFURTER CASSEROLE ALA TOBY

2 (1 pound) cans of baked beans
1 envelope onion soup mix
⅓ cup ketchup
¼ cup water
2 tablespoons brown sugar
1 tablespoon prepared mustard
2 teaspoons sweet relish
6 frankfurters, sliced

Mix all ingredients together and place in casserole. Bake 20-30
minutes uncovered at 350°. Serve.

●○●

MEATLESS CHOW MEIN

3-4 large onions, sliced thin
3 tablespoons oil
1 cup diced celery
1 can bean sprouts, drained (save some liquid)
1 can water chestnuts, slice in half
1 can bamboo shoots
1 can mushrooms stems and pieces
2-3 tablespoons soy sauce
2 tablespoons dark molasses
2 tablespoons corn starch
optional: any leftover turkey or chicken

Place oil and onions in large pot, cover and steam for 5 minutes. Add celery and steam again for 5 minutes. Add chestnuts, bamboo shoots, mushrooms, soy sauce, and molasses cook for another 10 minutes. Mix corn starch with liquid from sprouts and add to pot heat 5 minutes more or until liquid thickens.

TOAD IN HOLE
from Mary Thomson aboard "Ringers Rival II"

1 pound sausage
1 cup flour
¼ teaspoon salt
1 teaspoon baking powder
2 eggs
1 cup milk

Mix all ingredients and place in baking pan. Bake 15 minutes at 400°, reduce to 350° and bake 15 minutes more. Serve with cold applesauce.

QUICK GOULASH

1 tin of roast beef chunks
1 cup chopped onions
2 tablespoons oil
1½ teaspoons salt
1 tablespoon paprika
1 small can tomato sauce
2 cups peeled, diced tomatoes
2 cloves garlic, minced
½ cup gingersnaps, broken up
¼ cup warm water

In large Dutch oven pot sauté onions then add beef and gravy. In a small dish dissolve gingersnaps in ¼ cup warm water then add to meat mixture. Add tomato sauce, tomatoes, garlic, paprika, salt, simmer for 20 minutes. Serve over rice or noodles.

QUICK ROAST BEEF AND RICE DINNER
from Loretta Greene aboard "Boomerang"

1 can roast beef in gravy
1 cup cooked rice
1 large onion, sliced
1 green pepper, sliced
½ cup mushrooms, sliced
2 cloves garlic
salt and pepper to taste

Sauté onion, peppers, mushrooms in skillet with a little oil. Add roast beef and remaining ingredients. Serve with rice. I have even thrown in dried onions and pepper flakes when I have been in a real rush.

CHICKEN LOAF

1 tablespoon butter
1 small can mushrooms
1½ cups soft bread crumbs
1 cup milk
1 cup chicken broth
2 eggs
½ teaspoon salt
¼ teaspoon paprika
¼ cup cut pimiento
3 cups sliced cooked chicken

Mix all ingredients well and pour into greased loaf pan. Bake 350° 40-50 minutes. Serve.

CHINESE PEPPER STEAK

3-4 large onions, sliced
2 green peppers, sliced
3-4 cloves garlic, minced
4 tablespoons soy sauce
dash pepper
2 medium ripe tomatoes, quartered
2 tablespoons corn starch
½ cup water
¼ cup oil
1 chuck steak, cut into thin strips

In large skillet place oil, garlic and meat. Stir until all lightly browned. Add remaining ingredients except tomatoes, corn starch, ¼ cup water. Cover and simmer for 30-40 minutes. Mix corn starch and ¼ cup water and pour into mixture and stir until thickened. Add tomatoes stir lightly 1-2 minutes and serve with cooked rice.

CHICKEN AND CRAB DELIGHT
from Maggie Smith aboard "Water Music"

2 tablespoons butter or margarine
2 tablespoons minced green pepper
1 small onion, minced
fresh mushrooms, sliced (if possible)
1 pound deboned chicken breast, cut in small pieces
½ cup mayonnaise
½ teaspoon celery salt
1 teaspoon dry mustard
1 pound lump crabmeat

Sauté first 5 ingredients in a large frying pan until chicken pieces are done, only takes a couple of minutes. Add mayonnaise, celery salt, sherry, dry mustard and cook a few minutes more. Thicken with corn starch or flour if needed. Add crabmeat and stir gently. Cook until completely hot. Sprinkle with paprika and a little parsley. This goes together really fast. Serves 4 generous servings or the leftover is great for lunch the next day, cold.

QUICK STEW

1 pound hamburger or canned corned beef
2 onions, medium, diced
1 can baked beans
1 can vegetable soup
1 small can tomato sauce
½ package fine noodles

Sauté onions until lightly brown. Add meat and cook 5 minutes. Add beans, soup, 2 cans water and cook slowly for 10 minutes. Add raw noodles, tomato sauce and simmer until noodles are cooked. Serve.

○○○

CORNED BEEF STIR FRY
from Muriel Harnett aboard "Three Voices"

1 tin corned beef
1 tin kernel corn, medium
1 tin sliced potatoes, medium
1 medium onion, sliced
1 green pepper, sliced
dash salt and pepper to taste

In slightly oiled pan, lightly fry onion and green pepper. Add potatoes, corn, corned beef (broken up), add salt and pepper and stir fry thoroughly. Serves 3-4.

ONE DISH VEGETABLE PIZZA

2 cups biscuit mix
½ cup water
1 large onion, sliced thin
1 large green pepper, sliced thin
1 cup mushrooms, sliced
¼ cup olives, sliced
1 medium jar pizza sauce
½ teaspoon oregano
¼ teaspoon basil
¼ teaspoon Italian seasoning
¼ teaspoon salt
2 teaspoons garlic, minced
8 ounces mozzarella cheese, grated

In bowl combine biscuit mix and water. Mix well, and spread onto baking pan and let sit while preparing vegetable toppings. Add remaining ingredients one at a time spreading evenly. Bake 350° for 30-40 minutes.

⚬⚬⚬⚬⚬⚬⚬⚬⚬⚬⚬⚬⚬⚬⚬⚬⚬⚬⚬⚬⚬⚬⚬⚬⚬⚬⚬⚬⚬⚬⚬⚬⚬⚬

SKILLET POTATOES PEAS AND FRANKS

from Norma-Jane Deland aboard "Norma-Jane"

1 large onion, sliced
2 tablespoons butter or oleo
4 medium potatoes, scrubbed and sliced ¼″ thick
1 teaspoon salt
⅛ teaspoon pepper
1 cup hot water
1 bouillon cube
2 tablespoons flour blended with ½ cup milk
1 package (9 ounce) frozen peas or 1 small can peas, drained
6-8 franks or canned Vienna sausage

In large skillet sauté onion in butter till tender. Stir in potatoes, salt, pepper, water and bouillon cube. Cover and simmer 10 minutes. Stir in blended flour; cook and stir until thickened. Add peas, top with franks. Cover and simmer until potatoes and peas are tender and franks are heated through about 10 minutes. Makes 4 servings.

SAILORS RAREBIT

from Helen Dodson aboard "Terrapin"

1 can tomato soup
1 teaspoon Worcestershire sauce
½ pound store cheese (your favorite)
salt to taste

Cut the cheese fine and cook with tomato soup until creamy. Serve very hot on crackers or toast.

SEAFOOD STEW

1 cup celery, chopped
1 onion, large, diced
2 cloves garlic, minced
¼ cup olive oil
1 cup water
1 large can whole tomatoes
1 small can tomato sauce
1 teaspoon salt
¼ teaspoon pepper
1 cup white wine (optional)

Use the seafood of your choice, chunks of filet of fish, shrimp, lobster, scallops. In a large pot sauté onion and celery in olive oil, for 2-3 minutes. Add remaining ingredients except seafood. Cover and simmer for 15 minutes. Then add your seafood and wine simmer for 5-7 minutes. Serve on a bed of rice.

CORNED BEEF MAERDYM
from Joan Russell aboard "Maerdym"

6 ounces macaroni or 8 ounces noodles
¼ pound American cheese, grated (about 1 cup)
1 cup milk
½ cup onions, chopped
1 (12 ounce) can corned beef, chopped up
1 can condensed cream of chicken soup
buttered crumbs, ¾ - 1 cup
garnish with parsley and sliced olives (optional)

Cook macaroni, or noodles, drain, rinse and drain. Combine remaining ingredients (except crumbs) and alternate with layers of macaroni in greased 2 quart casserole. Top with crumbs. Bake in 375° oven one hour. Garnish with parsley and olive slices, if desired. Serves 8-9.

CHICKEN NORMANDY

from Norma Henderson aboard "Cera"

**2 apples, peeled and sliced
4 tablespoons raisins
4 tablespoons honey
5 tablespoons cider or wine
1 chicken, cut up in small pieces
dash salt and pepper**

Place apples in a pie dish, place chicken on top followed by the remaining ingredients. Cover and cook in hot oven for 45 minutes, basting from time to time. Eat and enjoy.

ZUCCHINI FISHCAKES

**1 small can tuna or 1 pound can pink salmon
1 onion, medium, chopped
2 tablespoons butter
2-3 medium size zucchini, shredded
2 eggs
¼ teaspoon pepper
¼ teaspoon basil
dash salt
½ cup wheat germ
breadcrumbs to coat before frying**

Mix all ingredients except bread crumbs. Form into small patties and coat with bread crumbs. Heat oil in skillet and fry 3-4 minutes on each side until golden brown. Serve with a tossed salad.

○○○○○○○○○○○○○○○○○○○○○○○○○○○○○○○○○○○

CHILI CON CARNE

2 tablespoons oil
2 large onions, diced
2 green peppers, diced
1 pound hamburger or canned corned beef
1 bay leaf
1 large can whole tomatoes
½ teaspoon paprika
1 teaspoon Worcestershire sauce
⅛ teaspoon cayenne pepper
1 teaspoon salt
1 large can kidney beans (3 pounds, 3 ounces)
chili powder to suit taste

In large Dutch oven, sauté onions and meat until lightly browned. Add remaining ingredients except kidney beans. Simmer for 30-40 minutes. Add kidney beans with liquid and simmer additional 15 minutes. To stretch this meal more, serve over a bed of cooked rice.

CORNED BEEF STROGANOFF
from Nancy Primrose aboard "Tar Baby"

⅔ can corned beef, diced
1 onion, sliced or chopped
3-4 stalks celery, sliced thin
1 packet McCormick sour cream dressing
1 (4 ounce) can mushroom pieces

Cook onion and celery gently in a little butter, add beef and mushrooms. Make sour cream sauce using dry milk and juice from mushrooms and water. Stir in. Serve. Can make ahead and reheat.

CHICKEN STIR FRY ALA GYPSY

from Barb Bell aboard "Gypsy"

½ cup chicken broth
2 tablespoons sherry
1 tablespoon oil
2 tablespoons soy sauce
1 tablespoon vinegar
1 tablespoon sugar
1 tablespoon corn starch
dash ginger, red pepper
¾ pound chicken breast, thinly sliced
2 tablespoons water
8 oz. Oriental vegetables

Make a sauce of the first nine ingredients. Marinate thinly sliced chicken in two tablespoons of it for 10 minutes. Add corn starch to remaining sauce, set aside. In wok or fry pan heat oil, add chicken and stir fry. Next add Oriental vegetables with water, cover. Simmer 2 minutes. Stir sauce, add to wok. Boil 1 minute or until thickened. Serve with rice.

CORNED BEEF AND SPINACH CASSEROLE

1 can corned beef
1 medium onion, chopped
1 large can spinach, drained
1 small can coconut milk

In bowl mix corned beef, onion. then add spinach. Mix lightly. Pour into greased casserole dish, pour coconut milk on top. Bake 325° 15-25 minutes.

○○○

SKILLET LASAGNA
from Lucille Strubell aboard "Kool Kat"

1 pound ground beef
2 tablespoons margarine
2 cups medium noodles
1 (16 ounce) can tomato sauce
1 (4 ounce) can mushrooms
1 teaspoon salt
1 teaspoon sugar
¼ teaspoon black pepper
1 teaspoon garlic powder
1 teaspoon Italian seasoning
¼ cup chopped parsley
¼ pound shredded Swiss or mozzarella cheese

Brown meat in margarine. Stir in uncooked noodles and all other ingredients except parsley and cheese. Cover and cook over low heat for 20 minutes or until noodles are tender, stirring occasionally. Sprinkle with cheese, heat covered until cheese melts, sprinkle with parsley and serve. Serves 4.

QUICK CORNED BEEF CASSEROLE

1 can corned beef
½ cup bread crumbs or wheat germ
1 package dry onion soup mix
2 cups cooked white rice
1 small can tomato sauce
1 cup Cheddar cheese, shredded

Combine all ingredients in a large bowl, except cheese. Toss lightly. Grease a baking dish and pour mixture in. Bake 350° for 15-20 minutes. Add cheese, bake until cheese melts. Serve.

HOT CHILI

from Ann Ginsburg aboard "Semper Attempta III"

1 can corned beef, broken up
1 can jalapenõ pepper, cut into strips
2 large onions, diced
1 can red kidney beans, drained
1 large can tomato pureé
1 can tomato paste
½ can hot chili powder
⅓ - ½ can cumin
⅓ jar crushed red pepper

Place all ingredients in large 5 quart pot and simmer for 1 hour. Serve with yogurt on side and pita bread.

BAKED LASAGNA

½ package lasagna noodles, cooked and drained
½ pound hamburger
½ pound sausage, Italian hot/mild, your choice
2 eggs
1 pound ricotta cheese
1 jar marinara sauce, or your favorite red sauce
  (about 2 pounds)
1 package mozzarella cheese, shredded

In a skillet brown hamburger and sausage slightly. Mix eggs into ricotta cheese. Take a large baking pan and alternate layers of lasagna, spoonfuls of ricotta, meatsausage mixture and red sauce. Top with mozzarella cheese. Bake 350° until bubbly, 40-50 minutes.

●○●

MARCIE'S CASSOULET
from Marcie Cragg aboard "Marcie"

1 pound hamburger
1 onion, diced
1 green pepper, chopped
1 clove garlic, minced
pinch thyme, oregano, basil
1 (8 ounce) can tomato sauce
1 (15 ounce) can white beans
1 pound kielbasa, cut into slices

Brown in skillet the hamburger, onion, green pepper, garlic, add seasonings. Add remaining ingredients and simmer for additional 20 minutes. Serve with hard rolls. A can of pork 'n beans can be added to make the dish go further or if you have some real bean lovers to feed.

TUNA SALAD BAKE
from Lora Wandros aboard "Lora"

1 (10½ ounce) can cream of chicken soup
1 cup diced celery
¼ cup finely chopped onion
½ cup mayonnaise or salad dressing
½ teaspoon salt
dash pepper
1 (7 ounce) can tuna, drained and flaked
3 hard cooked eggs, sliced
1 cup crushed potato chips

Combine cream chicken soup (diluted), celery, onion, mayonnaise or salad dressing, salt and pepper. Fold in tuna and eggs. Turn into 1½ quart casserole, sprinkle with potato chips and bake in hot oven 400° for 35 minutes. Makes 6 servings.

EASY TACOS
from Karen Anderson aboard "Harmony"

2 pounds ground beef
2 cups water
2 (6 ounce) cans tomato paste
2 (¼ - 1¾ ounce) packages taco seasoning mix or 2 (1¼ ounce) packages taco joe mix
½ medium head lettuce
1 large avocado
2 large tomatoes
1 (7¼ ounce) can pitted ripe olives
2 (4 ounce) packages shredded Cheddar cheese
1 (9½ ounce) package corn chips

In large skillet over high heat, cook ground beef until well browned, stirring frequently. Stir in water, tomato paste and taco seasoning mix, heat to boiling. Reduce heat to medium low, and simmer 10 minutes more. Meanwhile shred lettuce, dice avocado and tomatoes, slice olives. Place these and cheese in small bowls. Spoon beef mixture into large bowl, and place on platter. Arrange corn chips and accompaniments around bowl. Each person can serve himself. Serves 8.

MULLIGAN'S STEW
from Lora Wandros aboard "Lora"

1 pound chopped meat
1 medium onion, diced
2 cloves garlic, minced
1 whole can tomatoes
1 pound macaroni elbows, cooked and drained

Sauté onions, garlic and meat in skillet until brown. Drain off fat. Mix in tomatoes and simmer additional 5 minutes. Add cooked macaroni into meat sauce and serve. Enjoy.

○○○○○○○○○○○○○○○○○○○○○○○○○○○○○○○○○○○○○○○

CLAM STEW
from Loree Alderisio aboard "Yesterday's Dream"

2 tablespoons butter
½ cup onions
½ cup celery
¼ teaspoon Worcestershire sauce
dash of Tabasco
1 teaspoon horseradish
1 large can of evaporated milk
2 (6½ ounce) can of minced clams (drained)
1 tablespoon of sherry

In a large saucepan sauté butter, onions, and celery until lightly golden. Then add Worcestershire sauce, Tabasco, horseradish, and evaporated milk simmer slowly, stirring often until thoroughly heated. Add clams, heat 3 minutes, add sherry, serve. Serves 4.

HASH SKILLET PIE
from Norma-Jane Deland aboard "Norma-Jane"

⅓ cup chopped onion
2 tablespoons cooking oil
1 (15 ounce) can corned beef hash
1 egg
packaged instant mashed potatoes to equal 2 servings
1-2 tablespoons milk (optional)
½ cup shredded sharp cheese

In skillet sauté onion in oil, remove from skillet when golden. Combine in mixing bowl with hash and egg. Pack mixture into hot skillet with spatula. Heat through. Prepare potatoes using enough milk to make them creamy. Spread over hash in skillet, sprinkle with cheese. Cook uncovered over medium heat for 10 minutes. Loosen edges, cut into wedges, serve.

◦◦◦

CHICKEN & VEGETABLES WITH VINAIGRETTE

from Lucille Strubell aboard "Kool Kat"

1 cup cherry tomatoes, cut in half
½ cup zucchini, cut in julienne strips
½ cup snow peas, diagonally sliced
¼ cup butter squash, cut in julienne strips
1 can (5 ounces) chunk white chicken
2 tablespoons wine vinegar
⅓ cup olive oil
1 teaspoon dried tarragon, crushed
1 medium clove garlic, finely minced
4 lettuce leaves

Combine all veggies in one bowl. Stir together and beat until well blended vinegar, olive oil, tarragon, garlic. In another bowl pour 1½ tablespoons vinaigrette over chicken pour remaining vinaigrette over veggies and refrigerate 1 hour. Arrange chilled chicken on lettuce leaves surrounded by vegetables coated with vinaigrette. Makes 2 servings.

HAM PINEAPPLE AND RICE

from Muriel Harnett aboard "Three Voices"

1 tin ham, diced
1 tin pineapple tidbits
1 medium onion, sliced
1 tin carrots, diced
1 green pepper, sliced
1 egg, slightly beaten
2 cups cooked rice
dashes soy sauce

In large skillet lightly oiled, place diced ham, onion, green pepper, sauté for 5 minutes. Add cooked rice, mix well. Add soy sauce, beaten egg, pineapple, and carrots. Heat thoroughly. Serves 3-4.

MOTHER MONA'S HOT DISH
from Laura Bristol aboard "Hope"

1 can corned beef
1 large onion, diced
1 bell pepper, cut up
1-2 stalks celery, bite size pieces
½ head cabbage in bite size pieces
1 can whole tomatoes
1 can tomato sauce
1 small can tomato paste (add two cans of water)
Dashes of fresh garlic, fennel, oregano, bay leaf,
   Italian seasoning to taste
1 glop of ketchup

Place all ingredients in large pot, cover and simmer until cabbage is done. Serve with fresh homemade bread. Serves 6.

EASY TURKEY QUICHE
from Cozy May aboard "Cat's Meow"

1 (6 ounce) package chicken flavored stuffing mix
1 cup chopped cooked turkey (or canned chicken)
1 cup shredded Swiss cheese
4 eggs, beaten
1 (5⅓ ounce) can evaporated milk
⅛ teaspoon pepper

Prepare stuffing and press into 9″ pie plate. Bake in 400° oven 10 minutes. Mix meat and cheese, sprinkle into hot crust. In a bowl beat together eggs, milk and pepper. Pour in mixture. Lower oven to 350°, bake 30 to 35 minutes or until center is set. Let stand 10 minutes. Garnish with tomato wedges.

Main Dishes

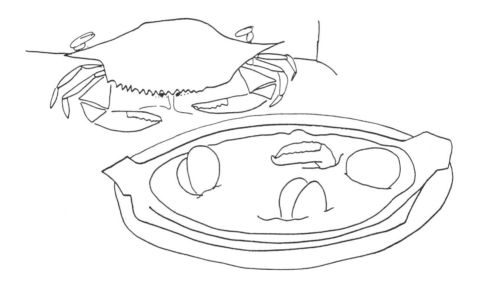

CHICKEN AND PEANUTS STIR FRY

2 chicken breasts, boned and cubed
2 tablespoons oil
½ tablespoon cornstarch
4 tablespoons soy sauce
1 slice ginger root, minced
1 green pepper, sliced
1½ teaspoons brown sugar
1 large onion, sliced
½ cup water chestnuts
½ cup mushrooms
2 tablespoons sherry
½ cup unsalted peanuts

Place cut up chicken in mixture of sherry, cornstarch and soy sauce. After thoroughly coated, heat skillet with oil and stir fry chicken mixture 4-5 minutes. Remove from pan and set aside. Next stir fry green pepper, onion, water chestnuts, mushrooms and ginger root. Cook this about 3-5 minutes. Add chicken, peanuts and brown sugar. Cook another 3 minutes. Serve with white rice.

JIM'S CHICKEN
from Betty Brock aboard "BJ III"

Skinned and boned chicken breasts
  (1 breast serves 2)
½ cup milk
½ cup seasoned bread crumbs
1 egg, beaten
1 cup Swiss cheese, grated
2 tablespoons flour

Pound chicken flat. In this order, dip chicken in milk, crumbs, egg, cheese and flour. Fry in butter 5 to 7 minutes each side.

ooooooooooooooooooooooooooooooooooooooo

MOM'S CORNISH HENS

from Karen Upham aboard "Loblolly"

2 Cornish hens, split in half
3 tablespoons butter
½ cup honey
1 tablespoon lemon juice
dash cayenne pepper
½ cup rose wine

Combine and simmer these ingredients. Sprinkle hens with salt, grill, basting with above sauce. (Can be made in a skillet.)

CHICKEN PINEAPPLE

6 chicken breasts
6 chicken thighs
¼ cup butter
½ cup flour
1 teaspoon salt
½ teaspoon pepper
1 can sliced pineapple, save juice
¼ cup soy sauce
¾ teaspoon ginger, ground
1 tablespoon curry powder
1 teaspoon dry mustard
2 cloves garlic, minced

In Dutch oven or large skillet with cover melt butter, add flour and stir until smooth, gradually adding the pineapple juice. Add remaining ingredients, except pineapple, and stir well. Put chicken pieces into sauce and simmer for 40 minutes. Add chunks of pineapple the last 5 minutes and serve with white rice.

●●●●●●●●●●●●●●●●●●●●●●●●●●●●●●●●●●●●●

CHICKEN LIVERS AND BACON

½ pound chicken livers
1 large onion slice
1 can water chestnuts
4 strips bacon, cut in small pieces
1-2 cloves garlic
2 tablespoons soy sauce
dash pepper
dash salt

In skillet sauté onion with bacon, then add chicken livers, garlic, soy sauce, pepper and salt cook medium heat 10-12 minutes or until livers are firm. Add water chestnuts, and cook 2 minutes. Serve on rice.

MANDARIN CHICKEN LIVERS

1 pound chicken livers
3 scallions
2 tablespoons sherry
1 tablespoon honey
2-3 cloves garlic, minced
3 tablespoons soy sauce
2 slices ginger root, minced
¼ cup water

Place all ingredients except livers in a shallow skillet and bring to boil. Place chicken livers into sauce and cook over medium heat for 15 minutes. Serve with rice.

CRACKER BOX CHICKEN

from Anne Freeman aboard "Rum Line"

2 chicken breasts
dashes salt, pepper, parsley and grated Parmesan
  cheese
2 tablespoons butter
2 tablespoons cooking oil
4-6 saltines crushed (or whatever has already
  crushed on the bottom of your cracker tin)

Roll chicken breasts that are split and boned into crackers, spices and cheese. Heat in a skillet two tablespoons oil and two tablespoons butter. Brown about ten minutes on each side. Serve and eat along with tossed salad.

ROAST CHICKEN

1 oven stuffer roaster chicken
salt
pepper
paprika
poultry seasoning
garlic powder
1 medium onion, sliced
1 stalk celery, cut into chunks
2 cups bread crumbs
2 tablespoons butter

In skillet sauté onion and celery in butter. Then mix this with bread crumbs and stuff bird. Then place bird in pan and sprinkle lightly with remaining ingredients and bake according to directions for size of bird. Remove bird let cool down for 10 minutes and remove stuffing, slice and eat.

PRESSURE COOKER CHICKEN

1 frying chicken, cut up in large pieces
¼ cup oil
½ cup water
1 large Irish potato, cut in quarters
1 medium butternut squash, leave skin on and cut in
   quarters
1 large onion, sliced
dash pepper
dash salt
1 tablespoon caraway seeds
2 tablespoons honey
2-3 carrots, peeled and cut in large bite size pieces

Place oil and onions in pressure cooker and cook for 2-3 minutes. Add chicken and braise slightly. Add remaining ingredients, cover and pressure cook for 15 minutes. Let pressure reduce on own accord. Serve with homemade cornbread.

HOMEMADE BURGERS
from Muriel Harnett aboard ''Three Voices''

1 pound ground beef
1 diced onion
1 egg
3 tablespoons flour
dash steak spice
salt and pepper to taste

Mix all ingredients. Form into patties. Pan fry.

QUICK SKILLET CHICKEN
from Norma-Jane Deland aboard "Norma-Jane"

2 whole chicken breasts (or boneless breast)
2 tablespoons vegetable oil
1 green pepper, cut into strips
1 small onion, sliced
1 cup celery, sliced
1 (5 ounce) can water chestnuts (optional)
1 vegetable or chicken bouillon cube in ⅓ cup hot
  water
½ teaspoon salt
2 teaspoons corn starch
3 tablespoons soy sauce

Split skin and bone breast of chicken or use boneless breast.
Cut chicken in strips. Cook in hot oil in skillet about 3 minutes.
Add next 6 ingredients, cover and simmer 10 minutes. Combine corn starch, soy sauce and add to skillet, stirring. Simmer several minutes. Serves 4.

HAM WIGGLE FOR TWO
from Gordon C. MacKenzie aboard "Piper"

2 cups white sauce (see page 182)
1 tin ham chunks or dice a small piece of ham (¼ - ½
  pound)
1 medium can early peas, drained
1 teaspoon celery seeds
toast

Prepare white sauce, add ham, peas and celery seeds, heat and
serve on toast.

SWEDISH MEAT BALLS

1 medium onion, diced
4 tablespoons butter
½ pound hamburger
2 slices bread
¼ cup milk or water
2 cloves garlic, minced
¼ teaspoon nutmeg
¼ teaspoon paprika
1 egg, beaten
salt and pepper to taste

Sauté onion in butter, add salt, pepper, brown slightly. Set aside. In large bowl add remaining ingredients, breaking bread in small pieces. Mix thoroughly and then add onion mixture, mix again. Form mixture into small balls and fry in ¼" oil turning to brown on all sides. Serve with your favorite sauce.

STUFFED PEPPERS
from Elizabeth Pollard aboard "Penobscot"

1 pound hamburger
1 medium onion, diced
½ green pepper, diced
6-8 mushrooms, diced, if desired
1 cup cooked rice
1 medium can tomato sauce
season with basil, oregano, salt and pepper

Stuff 4 peppers that have been cut in half, lengthwise with above ingredients sprinkle with Parmesan cheese. Arrange in large covered frying pan, add enough water to cover bottom of pan; steam until tender approximately 20 minutes.

TASTY CHUCK

from Art "Doc" Silvers aboard "Echo"

2-3 pounds chuck meat
1 can mushroom soup
1 package onion soup
water, about 1″ in pressure cooker

Cut meat in medium pieces, brown in bottom of cooker (then replace inner cooker rack, add about 1″ of water, replace meat). Then pour mushroom soup and onion soup mix. Pressure cook for 20-30 minutes, let pressure drop of own accord. The meat will be able to cut with a fork. Serve this dish with rice, noodles or mashed potatoes.

MEAT LOAF

2 pounds hamburger
1 medium onion, chopped fine
1 egg, beaten
1 teaspoon salt
¼ teaspoon pepper
½ cup wheat germ
1 tablespoon parsley
ketchup

In a medium bowl place all ingredients except ketchup and mix well with hands. Place mixture into a loaf pan and pack down. Top with ketchup and bake 350° 30-40 minutes. Serve. (If there's any leftover it's delicious the next day as a cold sandwich.)

oo

BAMI
from Loretta Greene aboard "Boomerang"

2 medium onions, sliced
1 cup your choice of three or more of sliced
   mushrooms, peppers, zucchini, spring beans, pea
   pods, broccoli
2 cups your choice — chinese cabbage, bok choy or
   cabbage
2 tablespoons soy sauce
2 cloves minced garlic
dash of pepper
3 packages Oodles of Noodles
1 cup cubed ham, chicken or beef
1 can bean sprouts, drained

Prepare Noodles according to directions, but retain only
enough liquid to mix with seasoning packet. Steam cabbage
and your choice of vegetables. In a hot skillet or wok, stir fry
all ingredients including steamed vegetables and noodles but
add bean sprouts at last minute.

GRILLED PORK CHOPS
from Karen Anderson aboard "Harmony"

Soak thick pork chops in Wishbone Zesty Italian dressing for
a few hours. Grill or pan fry.

ooooooooooooooooooooooooooooooooooooooo

SPICED BRISKET ALA TOBY

⅓ cup chili sauce
½ cup A-1 Sauce
dash Worcestershire sauce
½ cup water
4 pound brisket of beef
salt, pepper, garlic to taste
2 onions, sliced thin
2 tablespoons oil

In large Dutch oven place meat on top of oil and cook on high for about 3-4 minutes, turn heat down and add onions and remaining ingredients and simmer for 1½ hours. Remove meat, slice thin and return to pot and cook additional 30 minutes if you have a pressure cooker, cook meat on high heat for 3-4 minutes. Add remaining ingredients, cover and cook under pressure for 20 minutes. Shut off and let pressure drop of own accord. Remove meat, slice thin, return to cooker and simmer uncovered for 15 minutes.

FRIED CLAMS

¾ cup evaporated milk
dash salt and pepper
flavored bread crumbs
1 egg, beaten

In bowl beat egg, milk, salt and pepper. Dip clams into egg mixture and roll in bread crumbs. Fry in 2″ of oil 2-3 minutes or until golden brown.

NO BEANS CHILI

from Suzanne Stein aboard "Pleiades"

1½ pound ground beef
2 (16 ounce) cans tomatoes
1 green pepper, chopped
1 large onion, chopped
2 cloves garlic, minced
1 quart tomato juice
½ teaspoon thyme
½ teaspoon sage
1 bay leaf
1 teaspoon black pepper
¼ teaspoon cayenne pepper (or more for those who like it hot)
¹⁄₁₆ teaspoon Tabasco sauce (or more to suit taste)

In large pot brown ground beef with onion and green pepper. Drain excess grease. Then add remaining ingredients and bring to boil. Turn heat down to hold a slow simmer. Simmer for at least an hour. Then serve. Obviously the longer the chili is left to sit the spices get a chance to blend for a nice flavor. This is a good recipe for use in a crock pot.

CURRIED SHRIMP AND ZUCCHINI

2 slices bacon
2 medium zucchini, thinly sliced with skin
1 small can stewed tomatoes
1 can shrimp
½ teaspoon lemon juice
1/2 tablespoon curry powder

In skillet fry up bacon until crisp, remove and when cooled crumble. Meanwhile sauté zucchini in bacon grease 4-5 minutes. Add shrimp, tomatoes, bacon and seasonings cook for 2-3 minutes. Serve on a bed of rice.

GROUPER CAMELOT

from Miriam Field aboard "Camelot"

4-6 grouper filet pieces (marinate ½ hour in lime juice)
2-3 tablespoons lime juice
1 medium onion, chopped
2-3 cloves garlic, minced
4-5 tablespoons butter
1 small can mushrooms
1 medium can tomatoes
2 fresh tomatoes
1 cup tomato or V-8 Juice
hot sauce to taste
dash chives, thyme, salt and pepper to taste

Sauté chopped onion and minced garlic in generous amount of butter. Add mushrooms and cook a few minutes. Add grouper filet pieces, sauté lightly until opaque in color. Sprinkle with salt and pepper. Add tomatoes, juices, seasonings, simmer for 10 minutes. Let stand for 10 minutes. Serve with cole slaw or green veggie.

SHRIMP SWISS QUICHE

1 pastry shell uncooked
8 oz. can of shrimp (chopped)
8 oz. Swiss Cheese, cut into thin strips
2 tablespoons flour
2 eggs
1 cup evaporated milk
dashes of cayenne, salt,
2 tablespoons parsley

Toss cheese, flour and spices together then spread into pie shell. Beat eggs and milk well, add shrimp, stir gently, pour into shell. Bake 325, 40 min. or until set.

FISH FILET AND CORNMEAL BAKE

1 large fish, cut into filets
1 medium onion and green pepper, chopped
1½ cups corn meal
¼ teaspoon baking soda
¼ teaspoon baking powder
dash salt to taste
1 cup milk
2 eggs
¼ cup oil
1 teaspoon oregano
1 teaspoon basil
dash hot pepper sauce
½ cup shredded Cheddar cheese (optional)

In medium bowl mix together baking powder, soda, salt, corn meal, oregano, basil. Add onion, milk, eggs, oil, hot pepper sauce and stir lightly. Place mixture in greased baking dish and place fish filets on top. Bake 375° 15-20 minutes. Add shredded cheese, bake additional 5 minutes. Serve.

SKILLET FISH

from Loree Alderisio aboard ''Yesterday's Dream''

2 tablespoons butter
1 tablespoon oregano
1 tablespoon parsley
1 clove garlic, minced
1 tablespoon onion chopped (optional)
½ cup wine (White, Chablis or Trebiano)
1 teaspoon of fresh lemon juice
2 small fish (filet)
paprika (sprinkle lightly)

In skillet combine all ingredients except fish and paprika. Bring to a boil, reduce heat, then add fish. Sprinkle with paprika. Spoon sauce over fish occasionally till fish is done. Serve over rice. Serves 4.

●○

SWORDFISH STEAK ALA HENRY
from Henry Wagner aboard "Bookshelf"

6 swordfish, cut into 1" thick steaks
1 cup olive oil
4 garlic cloves, crushed
juice of 1 lemon
2 tablespoons crumbled basil
1 teaspoon celery salt
1 teaspoon black pepper
2-3 tablespoons melted butter

Combine all ingredients in large bowl, place fish into mixture and marinate for 2-3 hours. Cook on grill 5 minutes each side. Serve with a fresh salad and enjoy.

PAPER BAG FISH

4 whole small fish
salt and pepper to taste
1 teaspoon fennel seed
2 tablespoons butter
8 very thin slices lemon
12 sprigs parsley

Leave heads on fish. Sprinkle center cavity of each fish with fennel seed, dot butter, 2 slices of lemon, 3 sprigs of parsley. Wrap in old parchment paper bag, tie with string. Bake 350° 25 minutes. Take from oven place directly on plates so each person can open their own fish. Serve with rice and spinach salad.

○○○

COQUILLE CAMELOT
Scallops/Shrimp or Fish/Shrimp
from Miriam Field aboard "Camelot"

Bechamel Sauce: ½ to 1 cup per person
2 tablespoons butter, sherry, white wine, flour
2 cloves garlic, minced
1 small onion, minced
1 cup Half & Half or milk
1 bay leaf (broken in two)
¼ teaspoon nutmeg
1 tablespoon instant chicken bouillon
1 small can mushroom pieces, drained
½ cup swiss, jack or white parmesan cheese, grated

Lightly sauté onion and garlic in butter. Stir in flour, gradually add milk. Add bay leaf, nutmeg, bouillon, sherry, stirring till thickened. Add cheese and wine. Fold in mushrooms and seafood, sprinkle with parmesan cheese, slide under broiler until edges are brown or cover pan and simmer until fish is cooked.

CRABMEAT OR CRAWFISH FRITTERS

½ pound crabmeat or lobster
1 tablespoon minced garlic
1 tablespoon lemon juice
1 tablespoon black pepper
1 egg
1 cup biscuit mix (see page 67)
¼ cup milk
dash salt

In large bowl place flaked crabmeat or cut bite size pieces of lobster. Add remaining ingredients and toss lightly. In skillet heat oil, drop mixture by tablespoon and deep fry till golden brown.

TUNA FISH OR SALMON BAKE
from Linda Mailhot aboard "Lentetee"

1 medium onion, diced
¼ cup butter
1⅓ cups milk
¼ cup flour
2 cans tuna fish or one large can salmon
½ pound mushrooms in small slices
dash salt and pepper
1 teaspoon cayenne pepper
2 eggs, beaten
2 tablespoons cream
2 teaspoons lemon juice
1 cup cooked rice or toasted pieces of bread

Sauté onion lightly in butter. Add milk and flour, cook till thick. Add remaining ingredients, simmer for 10 to 12 minutes. Serve on bed of rice or toast.

CRABMEAT CASSEROLE

1 pound crabmeat
1 small can peas
1 can condensed mushroom soup
¼ teaspoon white pepper
½ cup grated cheese
dash hot sauce
1 tablespoon pimiento, cut in small pieces
1 tablespoon dry mustard
¼ teaspoon celery salt
paprika, sprinkle

Mix all ingredients and place into greased casserole dish, top with paprika. Bake in oven 350° for 20 minutes.

oo

BAKED BLUEFISH
from Barb Bell aboard "Gypsy"

3 pounds bluefish fillets
2 tablespoons onion, minced
dash salt and pepper
1-2 tablespoons mayonnaise
paprika for sprinkling
2 tablespoons lemon juice
Old Bay Seasoning if on hand

Wash and dry fish thoroughly. Put fish in single layer, skin side down on large sheet of aluminum foil. Place on shallow baking pan. Sprinkle fish with salt, pepper, onion and lemon juice. Spoon a thin layer of mayonnaise over entire fish. Sprinkle with paprika and Old Bay Seasoning. Loosely seal aluminum foil over fish. Bake, covered 40 minutes at 350° uncover fish and bake until lightly brown about 10 minutes. Serves 8-10.

HOT STEAMED SHRIMP

1 pound fresh shrimp, take off heads but leave shell on
1 tablespoon vinegar
¼ cup beer
water, enough just below steamer rack
2 tablespoons Old Bay Seasoning

In a large pot place steamer inside, bring ¼ cup of beer and water to boil Add shrimp and sprinkle Old Bay on top. Cover and cook until shrimp are bright pink in color about 4-6 minutes.

COCONUT SHRIMP

1 pound shrimp, completely cleaned
dash salt
1 teaspoon pepper
½ teaspoon paprika
2-3 cloves garlic, minced
½ teaspoon onion powder
¼ teaspoon thyme
¼ teaspoon oregano
¾ cup flour
½ cup milk
1 egg
½ teaspoon baking powder
1 (7 ounce) package coconut
oil

In a large bowl place flour, milk, egg, baking powder and mix well. Add remaining seasonings except coconut and oil. Dip shrimp into batter then coat thickly with coconut. Fry shrimp in hot oil until golden brown. Serve with your favorite sauce.

FISH BAKE

1 pound shrimp, crabmeat or crawfish
¼ cup mayonnaise
¼ cup flour
2 teaspoons curry powder
1 teaspoon lemon juice
¼ cup cream
dash salt and pepper

In lightly buttered casserole dish, place seafood. Whisk gently remaining ingredients and pour on top of seafood choice. Bake ½ hour. Serve.

HOT SHRIMP CREOLE

1 medium onion, chopped
1 medium green pepper, chopped
1 pound fresh shrimp or 1 small can shrimp
2 tablespoons oil
2-3 cloves garlic
1 small can tomato sauce
½ cup celery, sliced
¼ teaspoon cayenne pepper
¼ teaspoon basil
dash chili powder
½ cup water

Sauté onions, green pepper, garlic, celery, in oil. Add tomato sauce, pepper, basil, chili powder, water and simmer 10-12 minutes. Add shrimp, simmer additional 3-5 minutes. Serve over rice.

OYSTER FRITTERS

1 can (12 ounce) shucked oysters
1 teaspoon salt
dash cayenne pepper
1 egg
½ cup milk
1 cup flour
1 teaspoon baking powder

In bowl combine flour, baking powder, salt and cayenne pepper. Add beaten egg, milk and stir lightly. Let sit 5 minutes. Dip oysters into batter, fry in skillet 3-4 minutes or until golden brown. Serve with favorite sauce.

CRAB IMPERIAL

2 pounds crabmeat, preferably backfin
2 eggs
½ cup mayonnaise
1½ cups white sauce (see page 182)
½ teaspoon celery salt
⅛ teaspoon thyme
¼ teaspoon oregano
⅛ teaspoon dry mustard
1 tablespoon crushed capers
1 tablespoon pimiento, cut into small pieces
2 tablespoons green pepper, diced
paprika for topping, sprinkle

Mix eggs, mayonnaise, white sauce and seasonings in large bowl. Gently toss crabmeat into mixture. Place mixture into lightly greased casserole or individual shells. Sprinkle with paprika, bake at 350° for 30 minutes.

EASY SHRIMP CREOLE

½ green pepper
1 tablespoon butter
¼ teaspoon basil
¼ teaspoon oregano
1 medium onion, chopped
1 medium can crushed tomatoes
1 small can shrimp
1 cup cooked rice

Sauté onion lightly in butter, add crushed tomatoes, green pepper, seasoning and simmer 10-15 minutes. Add shrimp and simmer additional 5 minutes. Serve with cooked rice.

ⲟⲟⲟⲟⲟⲟⲟⲟⲟⲟⲟⲟⲟⲟⲟⲟⲟⲟⲟⲟⲟⲟⲟⲟⲟⲟⲟⲟⲟⲟⲟⲟⲟⲟⲟⲟⲟⲟⲟ

SHRIMP CREOLE WITH RICE

from Miriam Field aboard "Camelot"

4-6 slices bacon
2-3 onions, chopped
2 green peppers, sliced
2 tablespoons flour
2 (8 ounce) cans tomato sauce
1 cup water
4 ounce jar pimientos, sliced
1-2 cups ripe olives, green or black, cut up
4 cups cooked shrimp (1½ pounds)
4 cups cooked rice
salt, pepper, Worcestershire sauce to taste

Cook bacon remove from pan and dice. Brown onions, green pepper in bacon grease. Add flour, tomato sauce, water, and seasoning. Stir in pimientos, olives, shrimp, bacon and cooked rice. Simmer a few minutes and serve.

QUICK SALMON PATTIES

1 pound can pink salmon
1 medium onion, grated
¼ cup bread crumbs, or wheat germ
1 egg
dash salt and pepper
extra crumbs or wheat germ for coating before frying

Put pink salmon in medium bowl, discard the small cavity bones. Add remaining ingredients and mix lightly. Heat oil in pan, make patties dip for coating and fry each side until lightly browned. Serve with salad.

⊖⊖⊖⊖⊖⊖⊖⊖⊖⊖⊖⊖⊖⊖⊖⊖⊖⊖⊖⊖⊖⊖⊖⊖⊖⊖⊖⊖⊖⊖⊖⊖⊖⊖⊖⊖⊖⊖

MAINE LOBSTER STEW

from Elizabeth A. Pollard aboard ''Penobscot''

**2 small cooked lobsters, picked and cut into chunks
(save tomalley, liquid, white fluid and roe)
½ cup butter or margarine
2 cans evaporated milk
1 teaspoon sherry
1 shake nutmeg**

Melt butter in 2 quart saucepan, sauté lobster and roe until reddish in color. Add tomalley, liquid. Add milk, sherry, nutmeg, heat but do not boil, add more milk if needed, serve and enjoy.

CRABMEAT OMELET

**2 tablespoons butter
1 large onion
1 tablespoon parsley
½ teaspoon lemon juice
dash salt, pepper
dash hot sauce
2 eggs
1 tablespoon water
½ pound crabmeat, flaked**

In skillet melt butter and sauté onions lightly brown. In mixing bowl place remaining ingredients except crabmeat and mix well, add onions, flaked crabmeat and pour into greased skillet. Cook until firm. Remove from skillet, fold in half as you place on platter.

●○●

SWEET AND SOUR SHRIMP

1 pound shrimp, cooked (may substitute canned)
1 small can chunk pineapple
½ cup brown sugar
½ cup vinegar
2 tablespoons soy sauce
¾ cup water
2 tablespoons cornstarch
2 tablespoons cold water
1 green pepper, sliced
1-2 carrots, sliced

In small saucepan combine water, soy sauce, vinegar and brown sugar. Bring to a boil then simmer. In a small bowl stir cornstarch and cold water, add to hot mixture. Add green pepper, carrots and cook 5-8 minutes more. Add cooked shrimp and simmer 2 minutes. Serve with rice.

BAKED CRABMEAT AND SHRIMP

1 cup or small can crabmeat, flaked
1 cup or small can cooked shrimp
1 cup celery, diced
1 green pepper, diced
1 medium onion, diced
1 cup mayonnaise
few dashes hot sauce
¼ teaspoon celery salt
¼ teaspoon pepper
1 cup Italian seasoned bread crumbs

In large mixing bowl place all ingredients except bread crumbs and toss lightly. Place mixture into greased casserole dish. Sprinkle bread crumbs on top and bake 350° for 20-25 minutes.

SQUID & RICE

from Anita Pyle aboard "Conch Quest"

2-3 cans squid in ink, chopped
2 cloves garlic, chopped fine
1 sweet pepper, green, chopped
1 large onion, chopped
dash salt and pepper
hot sauce or hot peppers to taste
1 cup rice
1 cup water
oil

Cook onion, sweet pepper, garlic in olive oil just enough to fry till tender. Add chopped squid and ink, add rice and water. Cover and bring to a boil over high heat, then bring to low heat and simmer for 20 minutes. Let sit with cover on 10 minutes more before serving.

OYSTER RAREBIT

1 cup oysters
2 tablespoons butter
½ cup Swiss cheese, shredded
¼ teaspoon salt
dash cayenne pepper
2 eggs, beaten
dash basil
¼ cup water

Bring water to a boil and place oysters in, simmer for 5 minutes. Set aside. In saucepan melt butter, add cheese and seasonings. Slowly add eggs and oyster juice. Then add oysters and simmer 3 minutes. Serve over toast or rice.

INSTANT PAELLA

1 small can minced clams, drained
1 small can oysters, drained
1 small can shrimp, drained
1 cup bouillon
2 tablespoons minced onion
1½ cups instant rice
dash salt and pepper
¼ teaspoon parsley
2-3 cloves garlic, minced

Combine all ingredients into large saucepan, cover, bring to a boil, simmer 5-7 minutes. Serve.

CRAB CAKES

1 pound crabmeat
1 cup Italian seasoned breadcrumbs
¼ cup mayonnaise
¼ teaspoon celery salt
¼ teaspoon black pepper
1 teaspoon Worcestershire sauce
½ teaspoon dry mustard
¼ cup onion flakes
1 egg, beaten

In a large bowl mix all ingredients except crabmeat. Add crabmeat and mix gently. In skillet heat oil, shape into patties and fry on both sides until browned. For extra crunchy cakes, coat with breadcrumbs.

CRAWFISH ENCHILADA

from Anita Pyle aboard "Conch Quest"

2 crawfish tails, cooked and chopped
1 large onion, chopped
1 sweet pepper, green, chopped
4 cloves garlic, chopped fine
olive oil
2 (8 ounce) cans tomato sauce
1 teaspoon oregano
1 large bay leaf
dash salt and pepper

Sauté onion, green pepper, and garlic in skillet with olive oil. Add tomato sauce, oregano, bay leaf, salt and pepper. Cook over low heat till thick, then add cooked chopped crawfish about 2 tails. Simmer over low heat until tails are hot. Serve over rice.

SHRIMP AND RICE PATTIE

1 pound shrimp, cooked and cut into bite size pieces
1 egg
1 cup cooked rice
1 tablespoon butter, melted
dash pepper
1 teaspoon salt
1 tablespoon parsley
2 tablespoons water
flavored bread crumbs

In a medium size mixing bowl place shrimp, rice, butter, pepper, salt, parsley and mix well. In small bowl beat egg with water. Set aside and on a flat surface place bread crumbs. Make a pattie of shrimp mixture dip in egg and then crumbs, then fry until golden brown on both sides.

BLUEFISH SENAY

from Mary Carol Jones aboard ''Shadowfax''

1 pound bluefish filets, cut in 1" squares
1 teaspoon sesame oil
4 large dried mushrooms, can substitute fresh
   mushrooms
2 tablespoons soy sauce
1 tablespoon minced fresh ginger
2 cloves garlic, minced
⅓ cup dried lily buds (also called golden needles,
   optional)
1 tablespoon dry sherry
1 tablespoon cornstarch
3 whole scallions, sliced thin
2 tablespoons oil

Soak mushrooms and lily buds for 30 minutes in warm water
and then drain. Cut off hard ends and slice mushrooms thin.
In a small bowl, combine cornstarch, soy sauce, and sherry. Add
bluefish and stir to coat. Set aside. Heat wok or fry pan over
high heat. Add oil, when oil is hot, add ginger, garlic and stir
once. Add bluefish, soy sauce, sherry, cornstarch mixture and
stir fry until fish is cooked about 3-4 minutes. Add mushrooms,
lily buds and stir fry for 1 minute, adding 1 tablespoon water
if pan appears dry. Add scallions, stir fry for 1 minute. Stir in
sesame oil, serve over a bed of rice or cellophane noodles.

Pasta,
Potatoes,
Rice

CABBAGE AND NOODLES

from Kitty Haynes aboard "Hale Kai"

1 medium cabbage
1 medium onion
2-3 tablespoons butter
1 tablespoon caraway seeds
1 small package egg noodles, cooked
your favorite cooked meat, shrimp, ham, sausage
  (optional)

Sauté cabbage in butter with onions. Add seasoning and caraway seeds. Add cooked noodles to hot mixture and simmer 5 minutes and serve.

FETUCCINI

1 package fetuccini spaghetti
½ teaspoon salt
8 strips bacon, fried and cut into pieces
¼ cup Parmesan cheese, grated
2 egg yolks, beaten
1½ cups whipping cream
salt and pepper to taste

Cook fetuccini, drain replace in pot, add remaining ingredients except cream and blend well. Then add cream to mixture, take off stove, blend and serve.

BOILED LANYARDS

from Helen Dodson aboard "Terrapin"

1 package egg noodles
1 cup milk
1-2 cups ham, cut into bite size pieces
pepper and salt to taste
2 eggs

Boil noodles, drain add milk with slightly beaten eggs, ham and seasonings. Cook gently until slightly thickened and serve.

YOGURT NOODLE PUDDING

1 pound broad noodles
1 stick butter, melted
3 teaspoons vanilla
1 teaspoon salt
½ cup raisins
5 tablespoons sugar
5 eggs
1 pint yogurt, plain
½ cup cornflakes
½ cup shredded coconut

Cook noodles and drain. In large bowl blend eggs, salt, sugar, add yogurt, vanilla, raisins, and blend lightly, add noodles. Place this mixture into a greased pan. Mix in small bowl, cornflakes, melted butter and coconut. Spread on top of mixture. Bake 350° for 1 hour.

EASY BUTTER SPAGHETTI

1 pound package thin spaghetti, cooked and drained
¼ pound butter melted
¼ cup parsley
3-4 cloves garlic, minced

Cook spaghetti and drain. In same pot melt butter. Add parsley, garlic and cooked spaghetti, toss lightly and serve.

SKIN HOME-FRY POTATOES

4 medium potatoes, leave skin on
2 large onions, diced
¼ cup cooking oil
salt and pepper to taste

Wash potatoes, pat dry, and cut up in bite size pieces. Place oil in skillet and lightly brown onions. Add potatoes, salt and pepper, stirring occasionally until brown, tender but firm. Serve.

SCALLOPED POTATOES ALA TOBY

8 medium potatoes, sliced thin
¼ cup minced onions
1 cup milk
1 can cream of mushroom soup, undiluted
2 teaspoons salt
dash pepper

Alternate layers of potatoes and onion in greased baking dish. Combine remaining ingredients and pour over potatoes. Cover and bake at 350° for 45 minutes. Remove cover and bake 20 minutes more. Serves 8.

POTATO SALAD ALA BECKY

from Becky Aldrich aboard "Nel Fenwick"

4-5 potatoes
oil
oregano
vinegar
garlic salt, dash

Boil potatoes tender but firm. When cooled peel off skin and cut in bite size pieces. Add enough oil to coat potatoes then add to suit your taste oregano, vinegar, garlic salt. Onion and tomatoes can be added for color. Olives do well if fresh tomatoes are not available. Toss lightly, chill and serve.

POTATO SALAD LA FORZA

4 potatoes cooked, peeled and cut into bite size pieces
2 hard cooked eggs, sliced in chunks
3 scallions, sliced
¼ cup sliced olives, green or black
2 tablespoon chopped pimientos
1 tablespoon Old Bay Seasoning
½ teaspoon pepper
mayonnaise

Boil potatoes with skin on until tender, cool then peel and slice in bite size pieces. Place potatoes in large bowl and add remaining ingredients, mix lightly chill then serve.

ooooooooooooooooooooooooooooooooooooo

COOKED RICE

1 cup regular rice
2 cups water
pinch salt
1 tablespoon oil

Place all ingredients in saucepan and cover and bring to boil. Simmer for 15 minutes and turn off. Let cool down for 2 minutes and serve. This recipe makes 2 cups cooked rice.

FRIED RICE ALA CORINNE

1 cup cooked rice
2 tablespoons oil
1 large onion, diced
1 can water chestnuts, sliced
1 can mushrooms or use fresh if available
1 can bean sprouts
2 tablespoons soy sauce
1 egg, scrambled (optional)
½ cup diced cooked ham (optional)

Scramble egg and set aside. Sauté onion lightly in oil. Add remaining ingredients except cooked rice. Stir for 1 minute. Then add rice, egg and soy sauce. Stir thoroughly and continue cooking 2 minutes. Serve.

QUICK AND EASY FRIED RICE
from Loretta Greene aboard "Boomerang"

1-2 onions, sliced thin
1 pound cubed ham (or chicken or beef)
2 cups cooked rice
1 package dry onion soup mix
2 cloves garlic
salt and pepper to taste
serve with fried egg on top (optional)

Sauté onion in large frying pan or wok. Add remaining ingredients. Toss thoroughly and serve.

BROCCOLI CHEESE & RICE CASSEROLE
from Betty Brock aboard "BJ III"

½ stick butter or margarine
1 onion, diced
1 package frozen broccoli, cooked
1 can mushroom soup
1 cup grated Cheddar cheese
1 cup Minute Rice
1 cup liquid (½ cup milk & ½ cup water)

Sauté onion in butter. Mix all ingredients in baking dish. Bake 350° ½ hour. Serve.

GREEN RICE
from Angela Wellman aboard "Suffolk Punch"

1 egg
1 cup milk
2 tablespoons olive oil
½ cup chopped parsley
1 clove garlic, finely minced
1 small onion, minced
2 cups cooked rice
½ cup grated cheese
salt to taste

Place 2 tablespoons olive oil in baking dish, and coat evenly. In mixing bowl beat eggs and milk, then add the remaining ingredients. Pour into baking dish bake 350° 30-40 minutes. Serves 4.

ALMOST SAFFRON RICE

1 cup rice
2 cups water
1-2 pats butter
1 teaspoon turmeric

Place all ingredients into saucepan and bring to boil. Simmer for 15 minutes and let stand 5 minutes in pot before serving.

Vegetables

○○○○○○○○○○○○○○○○○○○○○○○○○○○○○○○○○○○○○

PORK AND BEANS 1-2-3

from Anne Ginsburg aboard "Semper Attempta III"

3 cans Progresso black beans, drain only 2 cans
1-2 cans pork, skinned and drained
¼ teaspoon thyme
dash corn oil

Put all ingredients in saucepan and heat slowly for ½ hour. Add more corn oil to thicken, serve.

KOSHER DILL PICKLES

Wash fresh cucumbers and pack in jars. Fill salt and
   water solution as follows:
2 tablespoons kosher salt or ½ cup sea water for each
   quart of water boiled and cooled.

Add a few heads of dill and 1 clove garlic, sliced fine for each quart, then seal. Stand in the sun for about 2 days until cloudy. Store in cool bilge.

PECANS AND ZUCCHINI

3-4 medium zucchini, cut into chunks
½ cup butter
½ cup chopped pecans
salt and pepper to taste

Steam zucchini just enough to be crunchy, remove excess water, add remaining ingredients, toss lightly and serve.

FALAFELS
from Linda Romano aboard "Peregrine"

1 large can chick peas, drained and mashed
3 cloves garlic, crushed
1 tablespoon dried parsley
⅓ cup water
1 tablespoon flour
½ teaspoon baking soda
1 - 1½ slices bread, in bits
1 egg, beaten
½ teaspoon salt
¼ teaspoon each pepper, cumin, basil
½ tablespoon oil

Mix all ingredients together well. By the teaspoonful, roll in flour. Fry in deep oil until well browned. Drain and serve. This is messy so keep fingers coated in flour whilst rolling the mixture — it's sticky.

ONE DISH VEGGIES

1 cup carrots, diced
1 cup celery, diced
2 cups pre-cooked rice
1 cup onion, diced
2 tablespoons oil
2-3 cloves garlic, crushed
¼ cup soy sauce
1 cup leftover meat, chicken or fish (optional)

Stir fry in large skillet oil, veggies and garlic for two to three minutes. Add meat, poultry or fish and soy sauce. Cook an additional two to three minutes tossing often. Serve on bed of rice.

CORN BREAD CASSEROLE

2 large onions, chopped
6 tablespoons butter or margarine
2 eggs
2 tablespoons milk
2 (17 ounce) cans cream style corn
1 pound package corn meal muffin mix or ½ pound
   corn meal muffin mix and ½ pound jalapeño pepper
   corn meal muffin mix
½ pint sour cream or yogurt
2 cups shredded sharp Cheddar cheese

Sauté onion in butter until golden brown. Set aside. In large bowl add eggs and milk blend well. Next add corn and muffin mix blend thoroughly. In a greased baking dish spread layer of batter, then a layer of each of the following ingredients: onions, yogurt, grated cheese, continue layering and end with a layer of cheese. Bake 350° 35-40 minutes or until puffed and golden. Let stand 10 minutes before cutting. This can be served at room temperature as well.

UNCANNED GREEN BEANS
from Nancy Primrose aboard "Tar Baby"

2 can green beans
1 can water chestnuts, sliced
1 tablespoon or more instant minced dried onion
1 packet Butter Buds or 2 tablespoons butter or
   margarine
1 can French fried onions (optional)
McCormick salt and spice to taste

Drain beans, add water chestnuts and seasonings. Heat on top of stove. Garnish with French fried onions.

⊙⊙

FRESH VEGETABLE SALAD
from Betty Kick aboard "Half Moon"

¼ pound more or less depending upon the size of
  salad you want:
mushrooms
zucchini
cucumbers
peppers, red or green
tomato
broccoli flowerettes
cauliflower flowerettes
black olives
water chestnuts
carrots
scallions

This salad is a treat when fresh vegetables are available and
it keeps on ice for a couple of days. Cut the veggies into bite
size pieces, marinate in Italian dressing for a few hours before
serving.

HARVARD BEETS

2 cups diced beets, use canned beets
½ cup sugar
1 tablespoon corn starch
⅛ teaspoon salt
⅓ cup vinegar
⅓ cup boiling water

In saucepan place sugar, corn starch, salt, vinegar and water
cook on low flame. Then add diced beets and cook additional
2 minutes. Serve. (Use some of the beet liquid.)

⚬⚬⚬⚬⚬⚬⚬⚬⚬⚬⚬⚬⚬⚬⚬⚬⚬⚬⚬⚬⚬⚬⚬⚬⚬⚬⚬⚬⚬⚬⚬⚬⚬⚬⚬⚬⚬⚬

COTTAGE PIE

from Linda Romano aboard "Peregrine"

1 cup lentils
2 onions, chopped
2 cloves garlic, crushed
2 teaspoons herbs
dashes salt and pepper
4 Irish potatoes, cooked, then mashed with butter and
  2 tablespoons Italian Seasoning
1 can tomatoes, or paste or sauce

Soak lentils in water for a couple of hours, then cook till tender and most of the liquid absorbed. Mash well and set aside. Sauté onion and garlic in heavy skillet, add tomatoes, herbs, lentils, salt and pepper. Simmer about 15 minutes. Cover with mashed potatoes, with lid on skillet, cook on stove until heated through.

RATATOUILLE

1 medium eggplant, cut in small pieces
2-3 medium zucchini, cut into cubes leave skin on
2 green peppers, cut into strips
4-5 tomatoes, chopped
3 tablespoons flour
½ cup olive oil
1 large onion, sliced
3-4 cloves garlic, minced
1 small can V-8 Juice
salt and pepper to taste

In large pan, heat oil, add onion, garlic and sauté lightly. In separate bowl, toss eggplant, peppers and zucchini with flour, then add to onions and cook for 5 minutes. Then add remaining ingredients and simmer for 40 minutes. Serve.

SAUTÉ ZUCCHINI BITS

3-4 medium zucchini, washed and sliced
2 medium onions, chopped
2-3 tablespoons oil
¼ teaspoon oregano
¼ teaspoon basil
½ cup sliced mushrooms (optional)
Parmesan cheese to taste

In a large skillet add onion to oil and sauté lightly. Add zucchini, seasonings and mushrooms, toss lightly. When veggies are firm but chewy, add cheese toss lightly and serve.

QUICK BAKED YAMS

1 large can yams, mashed
½ teaspoon cinnamon
½ teaspoon nutmeg
⅛ teaspoon allspice
2 teaspoons brown sugar or honey
1 small can of crushed pineapple
¼ cup raisins
¼ cup chopped nuts
6 marshmallows (or more)
¼ cup rum (optional)

In large bowl mash yams, add remaining ingredients except marshmallows and stir lightly. Place into greased casserole dish. Bake 375° for 15-20 minutes. Top with marshmallows the last 5 minutes.

EGGPLANT CASSEROLE

1-2 eggplants (don't peel), sliced into thin slices
2 green peppers, sliced
1 can crushed Italian tomatoes
salt and pepper to taste
1 can tomato sauce
¼ cup oil
1 teaspoon basil
3 strips bacon

In a greased casserole dish alternate layers of green pepper and eggplant. In a bowl mix tomatoes, salt, pepper, basil and pour on top of eggplant and green pepper mixture. Place bacon on top and bake 350° for 1 hour. Serve.

ZUCCHINI AND CHEESE CASSROLE

1½ - 2 pounds zucchini, cut into chunks
1 medium onion, chopped
1½ cups cooked rice
1 can condensed mushroom soup
1 teaspoon oregano
1 teaspoon basil
dash salt
¼ teaspoon garlic or 1 clove garlic, minced
1 cup cottage cheese
1 cup shredded Cheddar cheese

Mix all ingredients in large bowl except zucchini and cottage and Cheddar cheese. In greased casserole alternate layers of mixed mixture with zucchini and both cheeses save a layer of Cheddar cheese for top. Bake 375° 30-40 minutes. Serve.

TOFU ALA HELEN

from Helen Owen aboard ''Hel's Belle's III''

2 blocks tofu
¼ cup butter
4 tablespoons soy sauce
1 medium onion, sliced
1 green pepper, sliced
1 cup fresh or canned mushrooms, sliced
optional: fresh summer squash or zucchini or thinly
  sliced carrots
¼ cup water

Wash, drain and pat dry the tofu. Slice tofu, marinate in soy sauce 15 minutes, turning occasionally. Sauté vegetables in butter. Remove from skillet. Place tofu in remaining butter and brown. Add back vegetables and ¼ cup water with desired seasonings. Cover and steam 20 minutes on low heat. Seasonings can be curry, Italian or whatever.

HERITAGE WALSH CARROTS

from Lois Walsh aboard ''Pamlico Prowler''

1 pound package carrots cut into 1-2″ strips
½ cup sugar
½ cup milk
2 tablespoons parsley

Put carrots in medium saucepan with sugar and cook until carrots are tender. Then add milk and parsley and cook until liquid is thick. Serve.

○○○○○○○○○○○○○○○○○○○○○○○○○○○○○○○○○○○○○○

HOMEMADE PICKLED BEETS

1 jar sliced beets
¼ cup vinegar
salt and pepper to taste
1 medium onion, sliced thin
1 tablespoon honey

Simmer all liquid from beets with vinegar, spices and honey for 3 minutes. In larger container mix onions and beets, pour hot mixture on. Chill and serve.

PICKLED CABBAGE

1 small cabbage
½ teaspoon salt
1 cup sugar or honey
½ cup apple cider vinegar

Slice cabbage into strips put in mixing bowl. Combine remaining ingredients into saucepan and boil for 1 minute, pour over cabbage and let cool or refrigerate overnight.

QUICK OKRA PATTIES

1 can okra, cut into small pieces, save liquid
¾ cup corn meal
salt and pepper to taste
1 egg, beaten

In bowl place cut up okra, add corn meal, salt, pepper and egg. Add okra liquid to give you a pancake batter. Drop by large spoonfuls into hot oil and fry on both sides. Serve.

Dressings,
Marinades,
Sauces

SAUCES

Basic White Sauce:
2 tablespoons butter
2 tablespoons all purpose flour
¼ teaspoon salt
1 cup milk

In a saucepan, melt butter, stir in flour, salt. Add milk all at once. Cook and stir over medium heat till thickened. Continue to cook additional 1 minute. To the above basic white sauce you can create other easy sauces. Cheese Sauce: add ¼ cup additional milk. Add 1 cup shredded Swiss, Cheddar cheese into sauce and stir until fully melted. Serve over vegetables.

Zucchini Sauce: add fine chopped or shredded zucchini and cook additional 5 minutes. Serve on top of noodles.

Mexican Sauce: add 2 tablespoons of salsa sauce and serve over cooked pork or chicken.

Parmesan Sauce: add 2 tablespoons Parmesan cheese to white sauce and cook additional 3 minutes. Serve over vegetables, chicken, pork.

Sherry Sauce: add 2 tablespoons sherry and cook 2 minutes more. Serve over filet of fish.

Blue Cheese Sauce: add ¼ cup yogurt and ¼ cup crumbled blue cheese, and cook over low heat for 2 minutes. Serve over cooked vegetables.

MAKE EASY STEP YOGURT
from Joy Roherty aboard "Joy III"

1½ dry powdered milk (non-fat or with fat)
water to make 1 quart at 100°, from a boil
¼ cup starter

Mix well and then beat in starter. Pour into plastic or glass
containers such as left over margarine tubs, mayonnaise jars,
or new plastic containers having lids. Put the lids on and stack
the containers in an insulated box large enough to hold them
plus a quart jar of boiling hot water to keep the temperature
warm. Close the box and keep in a warm place 10-12 hours to
allow the yogurt to make. After this time, remove the yogurt
containers, allow to cool down about 30 minutes. Then
refrigerate until used. Save one container to "start" your next
batch. The yogurt is great plain, sweetened with sugar, honey
or jam and or served with lemon or lime juice. Bananas, canned peaches or pears with cinnamon can also be added and served as a salad or dessert. Yogurt may be substituted for mayonnaise in many recipes as well.

SOUR CREAM HOMEMADE

1 quart powdered milk
**½ cup buttermilk (powdered buttermilk comes in a
  tin)**

Place above mixture in a deep container, and let set at
temperature of 75-80° for 12 hours until mixture thickens
and sets. Another method that can be used is warm above ingredients and pour into a thermos and wrap in towels or place
in an insulated bag to maintain a warm atmosphere. When
the mixture has reached a jelly like consistency, pour this mixture into a cloth lined colander, and set over a large pan to
drain. Place the drained mixture in a container and keep
refrigerated for 6-8 hours until it is thick.

HOT BACON VINEGAR DRESSING

5 strips bacon
¾ cup cider vinegar

In skillet fry bacon crisp, remove from skillet. Lower flame on skillet with bacon grease and add vinegar slowly. While it is heating, crumble bacon and sprinkle on fresh spinach. Pour hot vinegar on top of fresh spinach and eat immediately.

CELERY SEED DRESSING
from Bonnie McDonald aboard "Bonnie Bird"

2½ cups sugar
1 quart oil
1⅓ cups vinegar
4 teaspoons salt
4 tablespoons prepared mustard
2 tablespoons dried onions
1 tablespoon celery seed

Beat sugar, mustard, salt, onion, and half of the vinegar till thoroughly mixed. Add oil gradually, then remaining vinegar, next celery seed. Makes 2 quarts.

YOGURT DRESSING

1 cup plain yogurt
1 teaspoon basil
2 tablespoons mayonnaise
1 tablespoon oil
dash salt and pepper
1 tablespoon honey

Mix all ingredients, pour on your favorite mix greens.

FISH BUTTER

½ pound butter
dash salt
1 tablespoon parsley
2 cloves garlic, minced
dash Worcestershire sauce
½ teaspoon lemon juice
¼ cup sherry wine

Combine together all ingredients and place in glass jar and keep in refrigerator. Use when you go to sauté that fresh catch of fish of the day.

FISH MARINADE

½ cup soy sauce
½ cup white wine
½ cup lemon juice
dash basil

Mix well, pour on fish, steam 3-5 minutes.

GREEK MARINADE FOR CHICKEN

1 cup dry white wine
½ cup olive oil
¼ cup lemon juice
2-3 cloves garlic, minced
1 tablespoon honey
½ teaspoon rosemary

Combine all ingredients, add your favorite chicken parts, marinate for 1 hour. Broil your chicken.

HOLLANDAISE SAUCE

½ cup butter
1½ teaspoon tarragon vinegar
Use a double boiler pot, don't let water touch top
  boiler
3 egg yolks
4 tablespoons boiled water
¼ teaspoon salt
⅛ teaspoon paprika
1 tablespoon cream or evaporated milk

In lower unit of double boiler bring water to a boil then turn down on medium flame. Place butter in top pot and melt then add vinegar and 2 tablespoons boiled water, use a whisk for beating. Add 3 egg yolks and beat until it starts to thicken. Add remaining boiled water and continue to beat with whisk. Add remaining seasonings beat slightly and remove from heat. Spoon over veggies or poached eggs.

QUICK CREOLE SAUCE

1 small can tomato sauce
1 green pepper, diced
1 medium onion, diced
½ cup celery, cut up in small pieces
¼ cup cut up olives
dash pepper

Place all ingredients in saucepan and simmer until vegetables are done.

ULTRA-SPICY CLAM SAUCE FOR NOODLES OR RICE

from Susan Baggio aboard "Warana"

3 onions, finely sliced or diced
6 cloves garlic, crushed
1 tablespoon parsley
½ teaspoon ground nutmeg
½ teaspoon oregano
pepper to taste
2 cans (5½ ounce) tomato pureé
2 (5 ounce) cans baby clams or fresh if possible
1 tin anchovies

Fry onion, garlic in olive oil or butter till golden, add tomato pureé and spices and stir well, cooking slowly for about 5 minutes. Add tin of finely chopped anchovies, then clams (drained—use some of clam juice or wine to make sauce the right consistency), simmer gently for about 10-15 minutes. Add diced peppers or celery for extra crunch.

TEMPURA BATTER

from Jean Stukey aboard "Cat Dancing"

2 eggs
2 cups ice cold water
2 cups sifted all purpose flour

Place eggs in small bowl, beat thoroughly with wire whisk or rotary beaters; blend in water. Sprinkle flour over liquid and stir into mixture with whisk or beater until all flour is moistened. Batter should still be slightly lumpy. Makes 3⅓ cups.

STEVE COLORADO'S ARGENTINA SAUCE

from Cozy May aboard "Cat's Meow"

1 cup vinegar
1 cup olive oil
2 cups pureéd tomatoes
4 cloves garlic, crushed
2 tablespoons each: salt, paprika, chili powder
2 handfuls fresh mint or 2 dried leaves

Mix all ingredients well in blender (or by hand). Store in tightly covered container. Shake well before using. Needs no refrigeration. Will keep up to 3-4 weeks. Use as cooking or BBQ sauce.

SPAGHETTI SAUCE

1 large can crushed tomatoes
3-4 cloves garlic, minced
1 medium onion, chopped
¼ teaspoon oregano
¼ teaspoon basil
¼ teaspoon Italian seasonings
dash crushed hot pepper flakes
¼ cup oil
¼ teaspoon salt
1 tablespoon honey

In large saucepan sauté onion in oil, add remaining ingredients and let simmer 30-40 minutes. Pour on your spaghetti or macaroni.

❍❍❍❍❍❍❍❍❍❍❍❍❍❍❍❍❍❍❍❍❍❍❍❍❍❍❍❍❍❍❍❍❍❍❍

MEXICAN CHINESE SAUCE
from Joan Smith aboard "Atria"

¾ cup tomato catsup
¼ cup water
2 tablespoons salad oil
1 tablespoon vinegar (any kind)
2 tablespoons brown sugar
½ teaspoon oregano
½ teaspoon powdered or rubbed sage
¼ teaspoon garlic powder or 1 small clove garlic,
   minced
1 teaspoon chili powder
½ teaspoon salt or more to taste
1 teaspoon soy sauce
¼ teaspoon onion powder or ¼ medium onion, diced

Mix and pour over meat, saving ¼ out to add while cooking.
Marinate 2 hours or more.

SAUCES MADE WITH CANNED CONDENSED SOUPS

1 can condensed soup of your choice: mushroom,
   asparagus, tomato or celery

Heat without adding milk or water. If it is too thick for a gravy,
add a little milk or bouillon cube diluted in water. After the
condensed soup has been heated add sherry or dry white wine.
Salt and pepper to taste.

SPARE RIB SAUCE

3-4 cloves garlic, minced
½ cup brown sugar
3 tablespoons vinegar
2 tablespoons soy sauce
½ cup ketchup
¼ cup honey
¼ cup orange juice

Mix above ingredients until well blended. Pour over ribs and marinate for 1 hour. Grill the ribs. I have even placed ribs in pressure cooker and cooked for 15 minutes under pressure then let pressure drop of own accord. Eat and enjoy.

SPICY TOMATO FISH SAUCE

1 small can stewed tomatoes
1 large onion, diced
¼ cup oil
3-4 cloves garlic, minced
1 small green pepper, diced
1 cup picante sauce

In a small saucepan place oil and garlic, add green pepper and onion, sauté for 3-4 minutes. Add tomatoes and picante sauce, simmer for 15 minutes. This is a great sauce for the catch of the day.

Cakes,
Cookies,
Pies,
Special Desserts

HONEY CAKE

1 pound honey
2 cups granulated sugar
2 cups cool black coffee
1 cup oil
3 large eggs or 4 medium
1 grated orange
2 tablespoons lemon juice
pinch salt
nuts and raisins (optional), handful
2 teaspoons baking powder
2 teaspoon baking soda
2 teaspoons allspice
4$^{1}/_{2}$ cups flour
1 jigger brandy (optional)

Place all wet ingredients into large bowl, then add dry ingredients, mix well and pour batter into 11 x 14 Greased and lightly flour dusted baking pan. Bake 325° for 1 hour, test with toothpick for dryness.

BANANA CAKE

1 stick margarine
1 cup sugar
2 eggs
3 ripe bananas
2 cups flour
1 teaspoon baking soda
½ cup chopped nuts (optional)

Cream margarine, sugar, eggs, then add bananas and beat till creamy. Add dry ingredients and pour into 2 small loaf pans or 1 large pan. Bake 350° for 1 hour.

CARROT CAKE
from Mimi Layka aboard "Laykas"

4 grated carrots
6 teaspoons shortening
1¼ cups sugar
4 eggs, beaten
4 teaspoons baking powder
3-4 cups flour, add one at a time
pinch salt
top with jam, nuts, or raisins (optional)

Beat eggs, add sugar, shortening, baking powder, salt, carrots. Add flour one cup at a time. Place ingredients into greased pan, and add optional jam, nuts, or raisins or all. Bake at 325° until golden brown, 25-35 minutes.

APPLESAUCE CAKE

2½ cups flour
1½ teaspoons baking soda
¼ teaspoon baking powder
1 teaspoon salt
1 teaspoon cinnamon
¾ teaspoon nutmeg
½ teaspoon cloves
½ cup butter
2 cups sugar
2 eggs
1 (16 ounce) can or jar applesauce
¾ cup raisins
½ cup chopped nuts (optional)

In a large mixing bowl, cream butter, sugar and eggs. Add dry ingredients and applesauce. Mix thoroughly. Add raisins and nuts. Pour into greased loaf pan and bake 350° for 40-50 minutes.

CHOCOLATE CHIP COFFEE CAKE

1 stick butter
1½ cups sugar
2 eggs
1 cup sour cream
2 cups flour
¾ teaspoon baking soda
1 teaspoon baking powder
1 teaspoon vanilla
½ cup chocolate chips
½ teaspoon cinnamon

Blend butter and 1 cup sugar well, then add eggs, sour cream, flour, soda, baking powder, vanilla and blend again. In separate bowl mix chips, cinnamon, remaining sugar. Grease tube pan and pour half of cake mixture in sprinkle with chips sugar mixture. Pour remaining batter on top with chips again. Bake 350° 45-55 minutes. Test for dryness with toothpick.

DUMP CAKE
from Warren Coleman aboard "Cop Out"

1 can crushed pineapple
1 can cherry pie filling
1 box yellow cake mix
1 cup chopped nuts
2 sticks margarine
1 cup chocolate chips (optional)

Dump one can crushed pineapple into 11 x 14 baking pan, spread evenly (do not drain). Add cherry pie filling over pineapple. Spread evenly dry yellow cake mix over pie filling. Sprinkle nuts over cake mix. Slice margarine into pats, place over nuts, Bake one hour at 350°.

MYERS RUM CAKE

from Karen Upham aboard "Loblolly"

⅔ cup sugar
3 tablespoons Myers Rum
⅔ cup water
1 tablespoon honey
½ cup shortening
1½ cups flour
⅛ teaspoon salt
2 teaspoons baking powder

Combine sugar, rum, water, honey and shortening. Bring to a boil, cook until dissolved. Bring to room temperature. Stir into cooled mixture, flour, salt, baking powder. Pour resulting batter into greased and floured tins. Bake in a heavy saucepan (pressure cooker) with vent open. Pour an inch or so of water on the bottom and steam 40 to 50 minutes. A heavy cake that lasts forever on a boat if need be. It's usually gone before I have to worry.

JIFFY CAKE

3 cups biscuit mix
4 tablespoons shortening
1½ cups sugar
2 eggs
1 teaspoon vanilla
1 cup milk

In medium size mixing bowl, add first four ingredients and ½ cup milk and blend until smooth, then add vanilla and remaining milk and blend some more. Pour mixture into large baking pan. Bake 375° for 30 minutes.

LEMON GLAZE CAKE

from Joan Russell aboard "Maerdym"

1 lemon cake mix
1 (3 ounce) or small size lemon instant pudding
4 eggs, well beaten
¾ cup oil
¾ cup water

Topping:
2 cups powdered sugar
2 tablespoons oil
½ cup diluted orange juice

Beat first five ingredients, pour into 9″ x 13″ pan, bake at 350° for 40 minutes. Remove from oven and immediately poke full of holes with a fork (two inches apart). Mix topping ingredients, pour over cake while still hot.

TOMATO SOUP CAKE

1 cup sugar
1 egg
2 tablespoons butter
1 can tomato soup
1 teaspoon baking soda
½ teaspoon cloves
1 teaspoon cinnamon
1 teaspoon nutmeg
1½ cups all purpose flour
½ cup raisins
½ cup chopped nuts (optional)

In medium size mixing bowl, cream butter sugar and egg. Add tomato soup, soda and blend. Add flour, nutmeg, cloves, and cinnamon, blend again. Add raisins and nuts. Pour batter into greased baking pan. Bake 350° 30-40 minutes. Test with toothpick for dryness.

∞∞∞∞∞∞∞∞∞∞∞∞∞∞∞∞∞∞∞∞∞∞∞∞∞∞∞∞∞∞

SPONGE CAKE
from Linda Romano aboard "Peregrine"

2 eggs
1 cup sugar
¼ teaspoon vanilla
½ cup milk
2 teaspoons baking powder
1 cup flour
1 heaping tablespoon butter
grated rind of lemon
dash of salt

Beat eggs and sugar, add flour mixed with baking powder, salt, add vanilla. Bring milk and butter to boil, add to mixture. Bake 20 minutes on medium flame in heavy skillet covered or 15 minutes in moderate oven until golden brown. When cool spread with jam. Sprinkle top of cake with confectioner's sugar.

SPICE CAKE

½ cup butter
2 eggs
1 cup sugar
2 cups all purpose flour
2 teaspoons baking powder
½ teaspoon cinnamon
½ teaspoon nutmeg
¼ teaspoon allspice
¼ teaspoon salt
¾ cup milk

Cream butter and sugar in large bowl. Add eggs, then add remaining ingredients. Pour into greased baking pan. Bake 350° 30-40 minutes.

RICE CAKE

1 cup white rice
1 stick butter
½ cup sugar
2 cups milk
4 eggs, beaten
1 teaspoon vanilla
1 small can crushed pineapple

Cook rice and rinse with cool water, replace in pot. Melt butter and pour in bowl add sugar, eggs, milk, and vanilla, add pineapple, rice and blend lightly. Place in lightly greased pan and bake 350° for 1 hour.

NO BAKE CHEESE CAKE

3 ounces cream cheese
½ cup sugar
1 teaspoon vanilla
1 teaspoon lemon juice
½ pint heavy cream, whipped
1 graham cracker pie shell
1 can pie filling, your choice

Mix cream cheese, sugar, vanilla and lemon juice. Fold in whipped cream, put in pie shell. Place can of fruit on top and set in refrigerator. Do this early morning and serve at dinner meal.

PINEAPPLE UPSIDE DOWN CAKE

½ cup shortening
1 cup brown sugar
1 medium can sliced pineapple, save ½ cup juice for
  blending
¾ cup sugar
1 egg
1½ cups all purpose flour
½ teaspoon salt
2 teaspoons baking powder

Melt ¼ cup shortening and pour into baking pan. Then spread evenly on bottom of pan brown sugar, place slices of pineapple on top. In medium bowl blend the following ingredients, shortening, sugar, flour, salt, baking powder and juice. Pour batter on top of pineapple slices. Bake 350° for 30 minutes while hot, turn out of pan onto cake dish.

GRANOLA COOKIES
from Helen Caesar aboard ''Mel de Terre''

1 cup granola
¾ cup flour
½ cup soft butter or margarine
⅓ cup sugar
¼ cup brown sugar
½ teaspoon salt, baking soda, vanilla
1 egg

Add raisins, dates, nuts, chocolate chips, or anything you want to increase volume. Mix all ingredients, and place on a greased cookie sheet by teaspoon and press down with drinking glass dipped in sugar (they will bake faster) 375° 12 minutes.

SAUCEPAN BROWNIES

from Alice Allchin aboard "Piwacket"

⅓ cup shortening
2 squares chocolate
1 cup white sugar
2 eggs
¾ cup flour
⅓ teaspoon salt
½ cup chopped nuts
¼ teaspoon vanilla

Melt shortening and chocolate in a saucepan, cool. Add sugar, vanilla and blend. Add eggs, one at a time blend after each addition. Slowly blend in flour, salt, then add nuts. Pour into greased floured 8″ x 8″ x 2″ pan. Bake 350° 35-40 minutes. (If teflon coated pan reduce heat 25°.)

MAGIC COOKIE BAR

from Loretta Green aboard "Boomerang"

1 stick (½ cup) melted butter or margarine
1½ cups graham cracker crumbs
1 cup walnuts, chopped (optional)
1 cup (6 ounces) semi-sweet morsels
1⅓ cups flaked coconut
1⅓ cups (15 ounce can) sweetened condensed milk

Pour melted butter into 13″ x 9″ pan. Sprinkle crumbs evenly over butter. Sprinkle chopped nuts over crumbs. Scatter chocolate morsels over nuts and sprinkle coconut over morsels. Pour condensed milk over mixture. Bake until lightly brown on top 25 minutes.

COCONUT OATMEAL COOKIES

1 cup whole wheat flour
1 teaspoon baking powder
1 teaspoon salt
½ teaspoon baking soda
¾ cup butter
1½ cups honey
2 eggs, beaten
1½ teaspoons vanilla
2½ cups uncooked oatmeal
1 cup shredded coconut
nuts and raisins (optional)

Blend eggs, butter, honey in large bowl. Add flour, salt, baking soda, vanilla, coconut, and oatmeal, blend smoothly. Add nuts and raisins (optional). Drop by spoonful onto greased cookie sheet. Bake 375° for 10-12 minutes.

GINGER SNAPS

1 cup molasses
½ cup butter
2½ cups all purpose flour
1 tablespoon ginger
1 tablespoon baking soda
2 tablespoons milk
⅓ teaspoon salt

Heat molasses in small saucepan and bring to boiling point. Add remaining ingredients in large bowl, add hot molasses and stir well, chill thoroughly. Place mixture on rolling sheet and roll as thin as possible. Put thin slices on cookie sheet and bake 350° until firm.

COCONUT NO-BAKE COOKIES

from Angela Williams aboard "Suffolk Punch"

4 ounces margarine
2 tablespoons cocoa
2 cups sugar
½ cup milk
pinch of salt
1 cup shredded coconut
1 cup chopped nuts
3 cups quick oatmeal

In a saucepan melt margarine, add cocoa, sugar, milk and salt, stirring over heat until dissolved. Remove from heat, add coconut, nuts, oatmeal and mix well. Drop spoonfuls on waxed paper and let cool. Eat.

GINGER HERMITS

3½ cups all purpose flour
1½ cups sugar
3 eggs
1½ cups raisins
1 cup butter
1 teaspoon cinnamon
1 teaspoon ginger
1 teaspoon cloves, ground
½ teaspoon baking soda
1½ cups chopped nuts (optional)
1 teaspoon vanilla

Cream butter and sugar, add remaining ingredients and blend well. Drop by teaspoon onto greased cookie sheet. Bake 350° 10-12 minutes or until well browned.

CORNFLAKE PIECRUST

1 cup cornflakes, crushed
¼ cup sugar
6 tablespoons butter, melted

In a mixing bowl, combine above ingredients and toss thoroughly. Press mixture firmly into a 9″ pie pan, chill or let set until firm.

KEY LIME PIE

from Loretta Greene aboard ''Boomerang''

1 can condensed milk
½ cup Key Lime Juice
1 container Cool Whip, small size

Beat condensed milk and Key Lime Juice until thick. Fold into ½ of the Cool Whip and place in favorite cooked pie shell, top with remaining Cool Whip, serve.

PIE PASTRY

1¼ cups all purpose flour
½ teaspoon salt
⅓ cup shortening
3-4 tablespoons cold water

Stir together flour and salt, cut in shortening. Sprinkle 1 tablespoon of cold water at a time, gently toss with a fork. Continue adding cold water one at a time until dough can be formed into a ball. On a lightly floured surface, roll dough from center to edge, forming a circle. Place in pie plate.

APPLE PIE NO SUGAR
from Helen Owen aboard "Hel's Belles III"

3 tablespoons cornstarch
½ cup orange juice
1 teaspoon cinnamon
nutmeg, dash
4-6 apples (pared, sliced to fill pie pan)

Prepare your favorite crust. Add mixture of cornstarch, cinnamon, nutmeg to apples. After putting apples into bottom crust, add orange juice. Add top crust. Bake 450° 10 minutes 350° about 25 minutes. Note: raisins or unsweetened crushed pineapple may be added for variety.

JUST CHEDDAR PIE

2 cups milk
1 cup Bisquick
3 eggs
¼ teaspoon salt
¼ teaspoon pepper
¼ cup chopped onion
½ cup shredded Cheddar cheese

Mix all ingredients in medium bowl except cheese. Add any leftover veggies, meat or fish. Place in lightly greased pan. Bake 375° 30-40 minutes. Add cheese on top and bake until melted. Serve.

STRAWBERRY YOGURT PIE

2 small containers strawberry yogurt, or plain and
  add strawberry jam
½ cup strawberries, fresh or frozen
1 container (8 ounce) Cool Whip
1 graham cracker crust

Mix all ingredients together and spoon into pie crust. Put in
refrigerator and let set 4 hours. Serve.

PINK CHERRY DESSERT
from Marcie Cragg aboard "Marcie"

1 can crushed pineapple, drained
1 can cherry pie filling
1 (4½ ounce) Cool Whip
1 can condensed milk

Mix all ingredients together and pour into bowl or flat rectangular container. Chill, then serve.

RUSSIAN CARAMELS
from Susan Baggio aboard "Warana"

2 ounces butter 4 T
1 tablespoon golden syrup (Karo)
¼ pound sugar 9½ Tablespoons
½ tin condensed milk
4 drops vanilla flavor

Put butter, sugar, syrup and milk into saucepan and bring to
boil. Stir well for 15 minutes. Add vanilla, turn out onto a
cookie sheet, mark into squares, cut when cool, wrap in paper.

BLOBS
from Barbara Muller aboard "IO"

1½ cups graham crackers, crushed
1 can condensed milk
1 package (6 ounce) chocolate chips
1 teaspoon vanilla

Grease 9" x 9" pan. Mix all ingredients together and spread mixture into pan. Bake 325° for 20-25 minutes. Done when cake tester comes out clean. Immediately remove from pan and place on piece of aluminum foil. Cut with knife (dip knife in hot water for clean cut). So named blobs because of consistency when mixing of batter and also what one will look like if one eats too many.

PEANUT FINGERS
from Phyllis Owen aboard "Prince Madoc"

½ loaf bread
½ cup peanut butter
⅛ cup cooking oil
2 cups cornflakes

Cut bread into ¾" slices and dry either by oven or in open air until almost dry. In a pan, combine peanut butter, oil and heat just until mixture is melted. Dip breadsticks into mixture, roll in cornflakes. Other crumbs or nuts can be substituted for cornflakes. Let set, then eat.

MAPLE NUT CHEWY BARS
from Jean Shaffer aboard "Gitana"

½ cup shortening
2 cups brown sugar
½ teaspoon maple extract
2 eggs, beaten
1 cup flour
1 teaspoon baking powder
¼ teaspoon salt
1 cup rolled oats
½ cup walnuts or pecans

Melt shortening, add 2 rounded cups brown sugar mixed with maple extract, and 2 beaten eggs. Mix well. Sift together flour, baking powder, and salt. Add dry ingredients to first mixture, beat well, then add rolled oats and chopped walnuts or pecans, mix well. Spread batter in square or rectangular cake or loaf pans, which have been greased. Batter should not be over about 1½" thick on pans. Bake at 350° till done — watch carefully and don't over bake. They should be chewy when cool, not hard or crisp. Cool in pans, then cut in squares.

WHITE CHRISTMAS
from Susan Baggio aboard "Warana"

1 cup icing sugar (confectioner's)
1 cup powdered milk
1 cup shredded coconut
1½ cups Rice Crispies
1 cup mixed fruit, or raisins, nuts, cherries
6 ounces shortening

Melt shortening (not hot) pour over dry ingredients squeeze well to mix, then press into a flat tin and put in a cool place. Cut into squares just before setting.

PRESSURE COOKER BREAD PUDDING
from Lora Wandros aboard "Lora"

2 cups hot milk
2 eggs, slightly beaten
3 slices bread, cubed
1 tablespoon butter
¼ teaspoon salt
½ cup brown sugar
½ teaspoon cinnamon
½ teaspoon vanilla
½ cup raisins
½ cup chopped nuts
4 cups water

Place all ingredients except water into a buttered bowl. Cover bowl firmly with aluminum foil. Pour water into pressure cooker, place rack in pot and set bowl on top. Close cover securely. Allow steam to flow from vent pipe for 5 minutes. Place pressure regulator on vent pipe and cook for 15 minutes with pressure regulator rocking slowly. Let pressure drop of its own accord. Serves 4-6.

CRANBERRY BAKED APPLES

6 apples, washed and cored
4-6 tablespoons honey
1 cup fresh cranberries
water, just enough to cover bottom of saucepan
¼ teaspoon lemon juice

Place washed and cored apples in pot, add water. Try to place cranberries into hole of apples first. Spread the remaining freely. Add juice and honey. Cover and simmer until apples are firm but tender when piercing with fork. Serve with cream (optional).

JAM TARTS

from Linda Romano aboard "Peregrine"

1 cup flour
½ teaspoon salt
⅓ cup shortening
3-4 tablespoons cold water
1 jar favorite jam

Sift together flour and salt. Then work shortening into flour with fingers. Add water one spoon at a time until dough holds together well. Roll out thinly. Press rings of dough with top of tumbler or similar utensil. Grease muffin pans and fill with rings of pastry and into each circle of pastry drop one teaspoon of jam. Bake in heavy skillet with lid for 20 minutes on medium flame until pastry is cooked. My muffin pans are cut so I can fit two sections one on top of the other in the skillet.

COCOA FUDGE

3 cups sugar
1/2 cup milk (or slightly more if needed)
3 tablespoons cocoa
1 tablespoon butter
¼ teaspoon vanilla
¼ cup chopped nuts (optional)

In saucepan place all ingredients except vanilla and nuts and cook until the following test. When dropped by teaspoon into cold water it will make a soft ball. Then remove from heat and place into bowl to cool down. Add vanilla and nuts blend in. Drop by teaspoon onto wax paper until firm and dry. Stores well.

CONDENSED MILK

from Phyllis Owen aboard "Prince Madoc"

⅓ cup boiling water
⅔ cup sugar
1 cup powdered milk
3 teaspoons margarine

Combine all ingredients and stir slowly until sugar is dissolved. Let cool down and store in air tight container in refrigerator.

EASY FRUIT CAKE

1¼ cups self-rising flour
2 sticks butter
1 cup sugar
1 tablespoon molasses
¼ teaspoon allspice
¼ teaspoon nutmeg
¼ teaspoon ground cloves
3 eggs
¼ cup dark rum or brandy
1½ cups fruit (raisins, dates, candied fruit like
   cherries, pineapple etc.)
powdered sugar (optional)

Cream butter and sugar. Add molasses, eggs, water and blend in. Mix flour, spices and add to mixture. Add the fruit and pour into large cake pan or two small loaf pans. Bake 350° for 1 hour or until cake is firm. Remove from oven and let cake cool slightly before removing from cake pan, sprinkle with some powdered sugar.

HONEY FLAN

4 eggs
2½ cups milk
¼ cup honey
1 teaspoon vanilla
1-2 tablespoons honey or maple syrup

In a medium mixing bowl, beat the eggs until foamy. In a small saucepan, heat the milk and honey together until just about to simmer, then add the vanilla. In a slow thin stream, beat the milk mixture into the eggs. Pour the mixture into a greased 9″ layer cake pan or flan pan. Place pan into a large shallow pan that has been filled with hot water to a depth of ½″. Bake at 325° for 30-40 minutes or until the center is almost firm. Glaze with the honey or maple syrup.

SOFT PRETZELS

1 package active yeast
1½ cups warm water
¼ teaspoon salt, regular
¼ cup kosher salt, for topping
1½ teaspoons sugar
4 cups flour
1 egg, beaten

In large bowl dissolve yeast in water, add regular salt, sugar, and flour. After mixture comes off of sides of bowl, place dough on flour surface and knead into soft dough. No rising necessary. Cut into dough and make small pieces and tie in pretzel shapes. Place on covered cookie sheet, brush with egg, and kosher salt. Bake 375° until golden brown.

CHERRY OR BLUEBERRY SQUARES

from Loretta Greene aboard ''Boomerang''

2¼ cups flour
¾ cup margarine
2 teaspoons baking powder
¾ cup sugar
1 cup milk
2 eggs
1½ teaspoon vanilla
1½ - 2 cans pie filling

Topping:
1 cup flour
¼ cup sugar
¼ cup batter

Combine flour, margarine, baking powder, and sugar. Work like pie crust until mixture looks like corn meal. Beat two eggs in a half cup of milk. Add egg mixture, vanilla and remaining milk to flour mixture. Pour batter into greased 11″ x 17″ pan (save ¼ cup batter for topping). Top batter with pie filling. Place topping mixture on top and bake 350° 30 minutes. Cut into squares when cool.

JAVA NUTS

from Phyllis Owen aboard ''Prince Madoc''

2 teaspoons instant coffee
¼ cup sugar
¼ teaspoon ground cinnamon
2 tablespoons water
pinch salt
1½ cups pecan halves

Combine all ingredients and bring to a boil. Boil for 3 minutes stirring constantly. Remove from heat, spread on wax paper, separating pecans as they cool.

COCONUT FUDGE
from Joy Roberty aboard ''Joy III''

3 cups well packed freshly grated coconut
2 cups sugar
pinch cream of tartar
¼ teaspoon ground cardamom
2 tablespoons butter
1 cup cold water

Oil a 9″ square or 6″ x 12″ pan, waxed paper or foil onto which to pour candy. Heat a large heavy non-stick surface pan over medium heat 1 minute, add coconut and fry, stirring constantly until dry and flaky but still white (5-7 minutes). Reserve in a bowl. Add sugar, cream of tartar to 1 cup cold water to the pan and bring to boil, stirring over medium high heat for 7-10 minutes until the syrup is thickened and becomes frothy. Add the coconut and cardamom and cook for 2-5 minutes stirring vigorously. Stir in the butter and continue to cook until the mixture begins to foam and stick to the bottom of the pan. Continue stirring to insure a flaky product. Immediately pour the candy onto the oiled surface and quickly spread evenly with a spatula (don't pack) then cut into squares.

PARTY DESSERT
from Helen Caesar aboard ''Mel de Terre''

1 package vanilla instant pudding
½ cup milk
½ cup strong coffee
whipped topping or Dream Whip
granola for topping, too

Mix pudding, milk, and coffee let set, then top with granola and whipped topping.

PARMESAN POPCORN

⅓ cup cooking oil
½ cup popcorn
Parmesan cheese

Place oil and popcorn into large pot with cover, pop corn. Place hot popcorn into large bowl and sprinkle with Parmesan cheese. Serve.

CREAM PUFFS
from Joy Roberty aboard "Joy III"

½ cup butter or margarine
¼ teaspoon salt
1 cup water
1 cup flour
4 eggs
instant puddings for fillings, your choice what kind

Place butter, salt and water into saucepan and bring to boil. Reduce heat and stir in flour until mixture leaves side of pan. Remove from heat. Beat in eggs. Drop on greased cookie sheet 8-10 puffs. Bake 375° 50 minutes slit sides and bake additional 10 minutes longer. Fill with your favorite instant puddings.

CHOCOLATE COCONUT DROPS

1 can condensed milk
2 cups chopped nuts
2½ cups shredded coconut
3-4 tablespoons melted baker's chocolate

In saucepan place condensed milk, add chocolate and melt. Let cool slightly, add nuts and coconut to mixture. Drop by spoonful onto lightly greased cookie sheet. Bake 325° 7-10 minutes.

OLD FASHIONED POPCORN BALLS

from Jean Stukey aboard "Cat Dancing"

5 quarts popped corn
2 cups sugar
1½ cups water
¼ teaspoon salt
1 teaspoon vinegar
1 teaspoon vanilla (optional)

Keep popcorn hot and crisp in low oven. Butter sides of saucepan, combine ingredients (except vanilla). Cook to hard ball stage (250° syrup will separate into two flow patterns from spoon with bowl tilted in horizontal pour angle), add vanilla - optional. Pour slowly over hot popped corn, stirring to mix thoroughly. Butter hands lightly and shape balls. Wrap if weather is humid. Makes 15-20 balls.

PIKELETS

from Susan Baggio aboard "Warana"

1 tablespoon sugar
1 egg
4 tablespoons flour
1 teaspoon cream of tartar
½ teaspoon baking soda
milk, small amount (see procedure)

Beat egg and sugar well, sift in flour, cream of tartar and soda, add a little milk until batter is consistency of sponge mixture. Drop by teaspoon onto a hot greased pan. Fry to golden brown on both sides. Great hot or cold with jam and fresh whipped cream.

APPLES AND JELLO

from Helen Caesar aboard ''Mel de Terre''

1 package Royal Apple Jello
2-3 apples, peeled and diced
1 cup diced ham (optional)

When a cold front descends make up Royal New Apple Jello and set out in the cockpit at night. At lunch time toss in diced apple and or diced ham. . . .What a nice treat.

TRAIL MIX

½ cup sunflower seeds
4 tablespoons golden or dark raisins or both
¼ cup unsalted peanuts
¼ cup shredded coconut
¼ cup chocolate chips

Mix above ingredients. Store in zip-lock bags for individual servings, or double the recipe and store in larger quantities.

◇◇

ⴰⴰⴰ

❝❝❝

220
INDEX

∽∽∽∽∽∽∽∽∽∽∽∽∽∽∽∽∽∽∽∽∽∽∽∽∽∽∽

222
INDEX

❦❦❦❦❦❦❦❦❦❦❦❦❦❦❦❦❦❦❦❦❦❦❦❦❦❦❦❦❦❦❦❦❦❦❦❦❦

ABOUT THE AUTHORS

Charles E. and Corinne C. Kanter enjoy the cruising lifestyle. Fourteen of their thirty sailing years were living aboard and cruising full time onboard their 32-foot catamaran, La Forza. Their cruising adventures are not only aboard their own boat, but delivering, charter-managing and racing through the East Coast of the United States, the Bahamas and the Caribbean.

The Galley **K.I.S.S.** *Cookbook*, a success since 1987, was revised in 1998 thanks to the support of its readers. The **companion** cookbook, The Cruising **K.I.S.S.** COOKBOOK published in October of 1997, is an entirely new and different format, adhering to the **K.I.S.S** principle.

Many lighter moments of their adventures are chronicled in their humorous non-fiction work: *The 13th Trip and Other Sea Stories* (where they change the names to protect the guilty!) Their latest book *Cruising Is Contagious,* is a compendium of their later adventures. In **CRUISING** *On More Than One Hull !* they detail the forty-one different catamarans and trimarans Charles has either sailed or surveyed. It covers 100,000 miles and twenty years of sailing experience. Charles' latest book, **SAILOR'S MULTIHULL GUIDE** *to the World of Cruising Catamarans & Trimarans* is the "Bible" of multihull sailing, according to world renowned French sailor/designer, Philipe Jeantot. It is now in it's second edition.

Corinne writes her columns, *Corinne's Culinary Corner* and *Cooking Aboard,* for several periodicals. Her recipes and her approach to cooking, Delicious, Nutritious, Economical and Convenient and the **K.I.S.S.** (keep it simple system) principle have traveled the seven seas. You can visit their web page at: <www.charternet.com/greatgear/greatbooks> or you can reach them by email at:<kisscook@sailcopress.com>

A COOKBOOK! A PERSONAL TREASURE,
A LOVING GIFT FOR FRIEND OR RELATIVE!

Ordered by:

Name: _____

Address: _____

City: _____ State: _____ Zip: _____

Telephone Number: (____) _____

Qty.	Title / Description		Price	Amt.
	The Galley **K.I.S.S.** *Cookbook*	@	$13.95	
	NEW The Cruising **K.I.S.S.** COOKBOOK	@	$24.95	
	Cruising, *On More Than One Hull !*	@	$24.95*	
	Sailor's MULTIHULL Guide	@	$29.95	
	NEW *Cruising Is Contagious*	@	$14.95	
	NEW *Tales From The Decks of Winddancer*	@	$ 9.95	
		Sub Total		
	* Special sale: $10 with purchase of any other book			
	Florida residents add 7.5% sales tax			
	Shipping: $3 first book, $1.50 ea. additional book			
	Total books	Grand Total		

Autograph to: _____

Mail to: _____

(if different than ordered by)

Name: _____

Address: _____

City: _____ State: _____ Zip: _____

Please make all checks payable to: *SAIL*co Press
P.O. Box 2099, Key Largo, FL 33037
(305) 743-0626 Tel & Fax

Credit cards accepted: ☐ VISA ☐ MasterCard (check one)

Number: _____ Exp. Date: _____

Name On Card: _____

*turn back one page READ ABOUT THE AUTHORS.

CHUCK
PRAGMATIC CAPTAIN!

CORINNE - INTREPID HEROIN
OUTRAGEOUS Go